THE
FOKKER
TRIPLANE

To Willy Gabriel and all of his kind

Jacket front illustration.
Leutnant Hans Kirschstein of
Jagdstaffel 6 flying Fokker Dr I
586/17 (Works No 2256), which
he named 'die optische
Taeuschung' (the optical
illusion). The angles of the
oblique black and white stripes
varied on wings and fuselage,
while the fore and aft stripes on
the tailplane and elevators were
the unit marking of Jasta 6.
Such was his success with this
system of disruptive painting –
his triplane was usually only
ever hit in the port wing – that
he continued to display this
style of marking on his later
Fokker D VII. Kirschstein
obtained 27 victories in less
than three months and was
awarded Germany's highest
military decoration, the Ordre
Pour le Mérite. He died from
injuries received in a flying
accident to a two-seat aircraft
in which he was the passenger,
on 16 July 1918.

1. Black-tailed Fokker Dr I of Jagdstaffel 12, a component unit of Jagdgeschwader II based at Toulis, near Marle in the VII Armee area, being flown for the benefit of the official Kogenluft photographer, March 1918.

THE
FOKKER
TRIPLANE

ALEX IMRIE

ARMS AND
ARMOUR

Arms and Armour Press
A Cassell Imprint
Villiers House, 41–47 Strand, London WC2N 5JE.

Distributed in the USA by Sterling Publishing Co. Inc., 387 Park
Avenue South, New York, NY 10016-8810.

Distributed in Australia by Capricorn Link (Australia) Pty. Ltd, P.O.
Box 665, Lane Cove, New South Wales 2066.

British Library Cataloguing in Publication Data: a catalogue record for
this book is available from the British Library

ISBN 1-85409-118-2

Designed and edited by DAG Publications Ltd. Designed by David
Gibbons; edited by David Dorrell; layout by Anthony A. Evans;
typeset by Ronset Typesetters, Darwen, Lancashire; camerawork by
M&E Reproductions, North Fambridge, Essex; printed and bound in
Great Britain by The Bath Press, Avon.

Also by Alex Imrie
Pictorial History of the German Army Air Service 1914 – 1918
German Fighter Units 1914 – May 1917
German Fighter Units June 1917 – 1918
Fokker Fighters of World War One
German Air Aces of World War One
German Naval Air Service
German Bombers of World War One

CONTENTS

▲ 2   ▼ 3

2. Genesis. One of the earliest examples of Fokker's first single-seat fighter to reach the front was the 80hp Oberursel U 0-powered M5K E5/15 (Works No 198) flown by Leutnant Kurt Wintgens with Feldflieger Abteilung 6b during the summer of 1915. This wire-braced monoplane used wing warping for lateral control and was armed with a Parabellum LMG 14 machine-gun firing through the rotating propeller via Fokker's Gestaengesteuerung (push-rod interrupter gear).

3. First production Fokker D V, 2710/16 (Works No 1068), raised into flying position and photographed at Schwerin, shows its clean lines. Based on Fokker's M22 design, for which Forssman/Bruening plywood wings were intended but not used, 200 examples of the D V were built. They were used only in non-operational roles.

INTRODUCTION

AMONG the manufacturers of fighter aeroplanes for the German Government during the First World War, the star of genius of the Dutchman Anthony Fokker shone with the greatest brilliance. Although its magnitude decreased for a period from late 1916 when Albatros products were in the ascent, from May 1915 when the German fighter aircraft was born, until the Armistice, the name of Fokker was synonymous with single-seat machines of this class. His development of the wooden cantilever wing is seen as one of the most important inventions in aeronautical science made during that war, and the first operational aircraft to use it in number was the triplane design that bore the company designation of Fokker V 5, the subject of this book.

Only 320 Fokker triplanes were produced for the German military authorities, and the impact of this type on the air-fighting scene was not great. It was, however, the best German fighter in the spring of 1918 and equipped the most famous fighting units, the elite Jagdgeschwadern, and as a result was flown by some of the legendary pilots. Almost without exception, the enthusiasm for this highly manoeuvrable machine was boundless, and although slower than the Albatros D Va, given the choice, the pilots preferred the triplane.

This is not a complete history of the Fokker Dr I: to cover that adequately would demand a far bigger volume. In a monograph of this type I have found it necessary to describe events that preceded the appearance of the Fokker triplane, in order to provide an essential background, and have also looked at some technical and operational aspects of the machine that may not be generally known.

The changes that took place in the display of national insignia, which transformed the appearance of the Fokker triplane and make it possible to determine the approximate date of the photographs, made it essential to present the photographs in a fairly strict chronological sequence. As a result, adjacent text may not always relate to the illustrations. The extended captions, however, tell their own story, and include information that could not have been embodied in the text without greatly exceeding the planned size of the book. If the captions contain repeated mention of the national insignia changes, pilot and unit markings, this is because the Fokker Dr I was at the front during a time when major changes took place in national markings, and was assigned to units whose operation depended on the display of easily recognizable markings. It was a highly decorated aeroplane and far more colourful than the black and white photographs, with which we are left today, reveal. The study of these markings has been a main interest of mine for more years than I care to remember, and has acquainted me with a number of triplanes, creating a personal allegiance that causes me to regard them almost as close friends.

The pilots wrote their names on their machines' stereotype factory camouflage finish by displaying personal colours or symbols, but the execution of these – now seen as a form of aerial heraldry – and the changes that were necessary to the national insignia were the work of the ground personnel; thus, although their names are generally less well known than those of the pilots, they too left their mark on the aircraft. But paint is only skin-deep and repainted aircraft tend to lose their identity; the Werkmeister (technical overseer) of the Jagdstaffeln, however, usually left more indelible imprints on their charges, these being occasioned by the necessity of maintenance, and some examples of the handiwork of these senior NCOs are mentioned in the following pages.

The use of many German words has been unavoidable, but translations are given at a first mention. It seems appropriate to introduce two of the terms here. The General in command of the German Army Air Service, from whose offices all orders and instructions of a military nature emanated, was the *K*ommandierenden *Gen*eral der *Luft*streitkraefte, or Kogenluft. Subordinate to Kogenluft was the vast organization concerned with the technical aspects of aeronautics, run by an inspectorate of military aviation, the *I*nspektion *d*er *Flieg*ertruppen or Idflieg. These two examples have been chosen to indicate how their use should ease reading without losing the impact of their derivative titles.

During my residence in Germany, I was fortunate to know personally the following men who had been intimately involved with the Fokker triplane, and I have thus been able to draw on a measure of first-hand information:

Hermann Becker (pilot in Jagdstaffel 12)
Walter Behrend (Udet's mechanic in Jagdstaffel 4)
Willy Gabriel (pilot in Jagdstaffel 11)
Alfred Greven (pilot in Jagdstaffel 12)
Hans-Joachim von Hippel (pilot in Jagdstaffel 5)

4. The Junkers J 2 all-metal cantilever monoplane powered by a 120hp six-cylinder Mercedes D II engine was an advanced concept for 1916. Made from 1mm thick iron sheet, the wings had no spars and obtained their strength from the wing's skin itself, which was reinforced internally by a second corrugated skin. Although strength was adequate, the necessary welded construction and type of material used meant that the aircraft was too heavy and its performance suffered as a result. While Junkers proceeded to overcome the weight penalty by using corrugated duralumin, Fokker sought to make cantilever wings entirely of wood.

5. Fokker V 1 skeleton assembly with two LMG 08/15 machine-guns installed. By employing deep box spars, which resulted in the use of a thick aerofoil section of considerable camber, Fokker developed the Forssman method of wing construction into cantilever structures. The small areas bounded by the rib flanges and the full-depth spars produced an 'egg-box' type of framework which, when covered with a skin of thin three-ply wood, glued and nailed to every member, gave an extremely strong wing that was stiff in torsion and in flexure.

6. Fokker in the cockpit of the V 1 in its original form. The rudder, which was probably blanketed by the downwash off the variable-incidence wing, was later raised by inserting a faired fin. The absence of this machine from the available list of 1917 Fokker prototype aircraft shows that the construction of this advanced aeroplane began before the end of 1916.

▲ 4

▲ 5   ▼ 6

Rudolf Klimke (pilot in Jagdstaffel 27)

Heinrich Maushake (pilot in Jagdstaffel 4)

Karl Riehm (Adjutant in Jagdstaffel 27)

Rudolf Stark (pilot in Jagdstaffel 34b)

Karl Timm (Voss's mechanic in Jagdstaffel 10)

A number of people have assisted with this book by making information available. Foremost of these is Peter M. Grosz, who has not only been a serious student of German First World War aviation history for many years, but he, more than any other individual I know, has been responsible for unearthing hard-to-find technical facts on the subject. In this he is seemingly untiring and is always extremely helpful in making his findings available to other workers. The Richthofen/Falkenhayn and the Fokker/Forssman correspondence, which supplies previously little known information that contributes essentially to this story, are examples of Peter's endeavour.

Another valued source was Manfred Thiemeyer, an active German researcher, who, not being content with already recorded information, contacts relatives of First World War German airmen to rescue from obscurity personal letters, diaries and photographs. One area of Manfred's interest concerns the origin of aircraft markings and he kindly made his findings available; these included, inter alia, the interpretation of the Voss engine cowling face marking.

Photographs, many of which are published here for the first time, came from a variety of sources, and apart from the above named, mention must be made of the following who kindly contributed: John Blenkey, Frank Cheesman, Ed Ferko, Dr Volker Koos, Museum fuer Verkehr und Technik (Berlin), Neal O'Connor, Peter Alting of Fokker Aircraft BV (Amsterdam), Heinz J. Nowarra, Bruno J. Schmaeling, Albrecht Vandenberghe and Etienne de Grave (Belgium).

Photographic interpretation has been an essential part of the preparation of the captions, and for this purpose first-class copies were necessary. As a hint of how demanding I was on Barrington Gray, who performed dark-room work on my behalf, there were many occasions when several prints in varying degrees of contrast were made from the same negative in order that the sought-for detail could be recorded.

Finally, I wish to acknowledge Joe Michie's artistic skill in his portrayal of Leutnant Kirschstein's Fokker Dr I 586/17 in the painting used to illustrate the book's dust jacket.

FOKKER FIGHTERS

IT was inevitable that Anthony Fokker, who had a keen inventive mind and was interested in all things mechanical, should have been attracted by the fever of aviation that was sweeping Europe at the time he had to decide on a career. He was born at Kediri in Java on 6 April 1890, the son of a Dutch coffee-planter who returned home to settle in retirement in Haarlem and to see his son educated. It was to complete this education that his father sent him to Germany in 1910 to study engineering. Fokker was able to enrol in a school for automobile engineers when he became aware that this institute was offering a course in aviation. Although apparently nothing much came of his attendance at this seat of learning, it at least laid the foundations for Fokker to construct his inherently stable Spin ('Spider') monoplanes and teach himself to fly. He qualified on 16 May 1911 when he successfully took the tests laid down by the Fédération Aéronautique Internationale and received the 88th Aviator's Certificate to be granted in Germany. At the end of 1912 Fokker Aeroplanbau GmbH was formed at Johannisthal near Berlin, but even before Fokker's enterprise was registered as such, it had become one of the most active flying schools in Germany, with a high pupil success rate, and its owner was by this time a skilled pilot.

Some Fokker 'Spiders' were ordered by the German Government and a number of Army officers learned to fly with Fokker, this being the beginning of Fokker's association with the German military authorities. By offering the Dutchman a long-term contract for the training of military pilots, the German Government caused Fokker to move his military flying school to Gorries aerodrome near Schwerin in Mecklenburg in June 1913, and it was there that workshop premises would expand over the following years to house the factory that was to become Fokker Flugzeugwerke mbH. Towards the end of 1913 several German aircraft manufacturers began to produce single-seat monoplanes similar to the very successful French Morane-Saulnier Type H. Fokker's M5 design retained some of the

▲ 7

7. Fokker with his revolutionary V 1. The small annular space in the front of the
▼ 8
low-drag cowling for engine cooling air to enter was possible due to the shape of the propeller spinner. Both these items were spun from aluminium and were 'engine-turned' to resist corrosion. The heavy beams on the wing under surfaces between the pivot bolts and the outer wing incidence operating rods were later discarded. The object on the starboard lower wing is a Morell direct-reading airspeed indicator of the anemometer type.

8. This fine action shot of Fokker flying his V 1, modified by fitting a vertical tail surface of increased height and area, shows to advantage the curved taper-chord profile of the engine cowling, which resulted in very low drag. This feature was further enhanced when the large diameter propeller spinner was fitted. It has been removed here, but due to its aerodynamic shape, engine cooling was considerably more efficient when it was fitted.

French machine's features and had, as a result, a similar appearance to the Morane, but was in fact engineered in a totally different manner, employing for example welded steel tube construction for the fuselage. Fokker, now recognized as one of the most highly skilled pilots of the day, demonstrated his aerobatic M5 to such an extent that he received several orders from private individuals, and after military evaluation of the type a number were produced for the Fliegertruppe. One version of the M5 had wings of reduced span, and it was to differentiate between this model and the normal version that the designations M5K ('K' meaning kurz or short) and M5L ('L' meaning lang or long) were introduced. These machines were, of course, unarmed and after the outbreak of war a number of M5Ks and M5Ls were used at the front for rapid communication and scouting duties.

For some time interest in several countries had been focused on using a machine-gun fixed to aircraft to fire ahead in the direction of flight, but on tractor designs this problem was compounded because of the rotating propeller ahead of the gun and various solutions were suggested. One of these, devised by Swiss-born Franz Schneider, the chief designer for Luft-Verkehrs-Gesellschaft (LVG) at Johannisthal, utilized an engine-driven cam operating a pushrod to fire the gun when the propeller blades were not in the line of fire. A patent for this system was granted to Schneider on 15 July 1913 (DRP 276 396), details being published in *Flugsport* magazine on 30 September 1914.

Apart from this public release of information, Fokker may have previously been aware of Schneider's work in this field, since it is known that he had informants within the LVG concern. Either or both of these sources could account for the experiments undertaken by Fokker at Schwerin late in 1914 to develop a method of firing a machine-gun through a rotating propeller.* It is not known what type of machine-gun was used in these trials, but it would appear that the main problem lay with the gun itself (or its ammunition) and not with the simple engine-driven cam and pushrod device used by Fokker, which was similar to that of the Schneider mechanism.

The first tractor aircraft to be used successfully in aerial fighting armed with a machine-gun firing through the rotating propeller was the French Morane Parasol Type L flown by the famous pre-war pilot Roland Garros, and its appearance on the Western Front caused consternation among the Germans. However, it was only a short time before Garros was brought down and captured on 18 April 1915. Although he burned his machine, the damage by fire did not conceal the fact that armoured wedges fitted to a specially shaped propeller protected it from the gun's bullets.

The adoption of a similar method for German aircraft without delay obviously gave the investigation of the 'System-Garros' a high priority, and his propeller and gun were sent immediately to Doeberitz near Berlin. However, even as Idflieg were formulating their requirements in this regard with the German aircraft industry, the surprising fact emerged that a device for firing a machine-gun through a rotating propeller already existed, completely ready for use, at Schwerin. Fokker was given one of the new air-cooled Parabellum machine-guns (LMG 14), fitted it to an M5K, and the modification and adjustment of this combination meant that only 48 hours elapsed before Fokker was able to demonstrate his armed aircraft to officials at Doeberitz. This machine, designated Fokker M5K/MG, was immediately ordered in quantity as the Fokker E I ('E' denoting armed single-seat monoplane or Eindecker) and was distributed to units on the more active parts of the front.

The success of the Fokker monoplane powered by the seven-cylinder Oberursel U 0 engine was immediate, and it was soon joined by improved versions, of which the Fokker (M14) E III powered by the 100hp nine-cylinder Oberursel U I engine was built in the greatest numbers. By the end of 1915 some 80 Fokker E monoplanes were at the front and air superiority was firmly in German hands. Initially dispersed among the two-seater units, the true value of the armed single-seaters emerged when they were operated in groups called Kampfeinsitzerkommandos (single-seater detachments – KEK); these temporary formations were the forerunners of the later permanent fighter units named Jagdstaffeln (Jasta). These aeroplanes, of which more than 400 were eventually built, made national heroes of their successful pilots like Max Immelmann and Oswald Boelcke, and established Fokker as an accomplished producer of fighting aeroplanes.

During the first six months of 1916 activity at Schwerin centred on a biplane replacement for the wire-braced E monoplanes which, although still in production, were inferior to the Allied biplane scouts that were beginning to make their appearance. Adopting a practical approach to the problem, Fokker produced a series of biplane designs to investigate by direct comparison the relative merits of single- and two-bay

*Personal statement from Walter During, Berlin, early 1960s. During, who was a mechanic with the Freiwilliges Marinefliegerkorps (Volunteer Naval Flying Corps) was positive about the period, since his service at Schwerin terminated in December 1914.

▲9

9. Work on the Fokker V 2
(Works No 1533) began on 7
March 1917, immediately after
completion of the V 1, and used
the 160hp six-cylinder
Mercedes D III water-cooled
engine. Because of this it was
heavier and of poorer
performance than its
predecessor. Note the attention
paid to fairing the engine: the

cylinder heads contained in a
helmeted cowling and the
exhaust manifold completely
enclosed within the fuselage
nose, exiting immediately
behind the propeller.

10. In an attempt to improve on
the performance of the V 2, the
V 3 (Works No 1610),
commenced on 2 May 1917,

had a greater gap between the
wings. It also adopted a normal
type of tail unit, similar to that
used on the Albatros fighters.
Richthofen considered the
Albatros D III rudder and
elevator controls to be good,
did not like the over-sensitive
'all-flying' Fokker elevators and
told Fokker so; Fokker
obviously bore this factor in

mind during the redesign. The
drag of the large Windhoff
radiator mounted on the centre-
section leading-edge and the
disruption of wing airflow that
it caused detracted from the
otherwise excellent
aerodynamics of this design.

▼10

bracing, wing warping and ailerons and stationary and rotary engine power. During this period a number of single-seat fighter types emerged and were awarded production contracts. They were all basically similar to each other, having two-bay wing cellules. They also bore great structural similarity to the earlier E monoplanes, being lightly constructed in order to obtain the maximum performance from the low-powered engines available. Using this method, Fokker obviously hoped to produce a suitable biplane fighter, but it appears that the style of construction employed had almost already reached its limit.

The Fokker D I ('D' denoting armed single-seat biplane or Doppeldecker) was powered by a 120hp Mercedes D II six-cylinder water-cooled engine and did not suffer such a severe performance loss above heights of 3,000 metres as aircraft powered by rotary engines of the Oberursel types; these, being built on the Gnome principle, used automatic inlet valves in the piston crowns. However, only one machine-gun was carried. The Fokker D II was basically the same airframe with slight modifications and powered by a 100hp Oberursel U I rotary engine with which it was underpowered and really lacked the performance required of a single-seater. A major disadvantage was that, again, only one machine-gun was fitted. A further modified version to take the 160hp Oberursel U III fourteen-cylinder two-row rotary was designated Fokker D III and was armed with two machine-guns, but the limitations of its engine made the type less desirable than the stationary-engined biplanes of the same power. Fokker's complaint was that he was denied an allocation of the 160hp Mercedes D III six-cylinder water-cooled engine, the power unit of the highly successful Albatros single-seater, but when he did modify the Fokker D I to take this engine and enable it to carry the desired two-gun armament to become the Fokker D IV, the airframe proved to be too weak. This was the price he paid for using flimsy constructional techniques in his constant battle to improve power/weight ratios. In fact, structural integrity was something that was to plague Fokker, and lack of it would manifest itself in various forms over the next two years. Now, in the autumn of 1916, the number of accidents to Fokker E monoplanes increased, and some of these were found to have been due to wing failure.

The above biplane types (D I – D III), for which substantial orders had been received, all reached the front within a short time of each other. They arrived in August 1916, coinciding with the formation of the first seven Jagdstaffeln, and were at the time the most numerous D-type fighter aircraft at the front, a situation that still obtained at the end of October when some 130 Fokker biplanes were with the Jagdstaffeln. But, with ever-increasing numbers in use, the frequency of accidents also showed a remarkable upwards trend. Investigation revealed that structural failure often proved to have been the cause, mostly brought about by poor workmanship, something that Fokker might have got away with on more robust designs, but this, of course, also reflected lax inspection discipline during manufacture.

Early in November it was considered that Fokker machines were no longer suitable for operational use. However, shortage of aircraft meant that a number of Fokker D types continued to serve at the front on quiet sectors and a further number were employed there on non-operational duties, but aircraft still on order were relegated to flying school work. The Fokker D I was deemed unsuitable even for school use and by late December 1916 a large number of them had been 'reduced to produce'. Against this background of despair, when Fokker's reputation rapidly went downhill, there was a faint glimmer of hope on the horizon. Fokker had apparently realized, despite the orders that he was receiving for the previously mentioned types, that the 'writing was on the wall' as far as his basic design and type of construction went, and in mid-1916 he created the last of the line of development that he had been following.

This machine was known by the company designation M22, an aircraft that was eventually ordered in series as the Fokker D V. Although it started life as an improvement of the Fokker D II, it possessed features that separated it from its fellows. Attempts were made to reduce parasitic drag in various ways. The forward fuselage had a good streamlined appearance, with curved sides and longitudinal stringers faired the completely circular engine cowling over the 100hp Oberursel U I into the flat fuselage sides aft of the cockpit. A large diameter aluminium spinner was fitted over the propeller boss, and this aided engine cooling by deflecting the airflow onto the engine cylinders before exiting through the open space at the bottom rear of the cowling. The wing cellule was of only one bay, thereby halving the number of interplane struts and bracing wires compared with those used on the Fokker D I – D IV types. To provide an excellent view for the pilot, the top wing centre-section, which had a large cut-out, was placed well forward and this necessitated a considerable amount of sweepback to keep the centre of lift in the right place. Destined to be used non-operationally because of the events already mentioned, the machine's speed of 160km/hr showed what could be achieved with low power when careful attention was given to creating

▲11

11. Although the German authorities had investigated the triplane configuration as early as 1916, the superior manoeuvrability and rate of climb of the Sopwith Triplane over the stationary-engined Albatros D III in the spring of 1917 caused Idflieg to evaluate the triplane layout further. The first example of the British machine to fall into German hands was N5457 flown by Flight Sub-Lt N. D. M. Hewitt of No 1 Squadron, RNAS, which forced-landed due to engine trouble near Mons on 6 April 1917. This is believed to be a photograph of N5457; apart from airframe damage, fabric has been removed, presumably to allow examination of its structure.

12. Fokker V 4 in its original form. This airframe, work on which commenced on 13 June 1917, started life as a biplane demonstrator for Austria–Hungary, but received a set of cantilever wings to become the first Fokker triplane. Note the use of simple unbalanced elevator and aileron control surfaces.

▲12   ▼13

13. The aerodynamically clean lines of the V 4 are apparent in this view. The loss of torsional rigidity due to the deletion of the plywood wing covering probably presented itself at this stage, but no steps were taken to rectify it since Fokker realized that an increase in wing area and more effective ailerons were required to improve performance.

an aerodynamically clean airframe. Apparently a delight to fly, the Fokker D V was to perform an important function during the transition of Albatros D V and Pfalz D III equipped Jagdstaffeln: it introduced their stationary-engined pilots to the different engine handling and flying aspects of rotary-powered aircraft when such units re-equipped with the Fokker triplane, and thereby doubtless reduced the number of accidents that might otherwise have occurred to this front-line fighter in the hands of novices.

THE CANTILEVER WING

ALTHOUGH Villehad Forssman, a Swedish aeronautical engineer working in Germany, had constructed a satisfactory small airship for the Russian Government in around 1911, at the Riedinger Works in Augsburg, his later ventures into heavier-than-air design were not entirely successful. He became involved with Prince Friedrich Sigismund at Bornstedter Feld near Potsdam on various monoplane projects, which culminated in the Bulldogge early in 1914. Attempts to improve the performance and handling of this machine at the Siemens-Schuckert-Werke after the outbreak of war, to allow its acceptance by the military authorities, came to nothing. Nor was Forssman any more successful at Siemens with the design of a large four-engined biplane bomber, based apparently on the Russian Sikorsky. Forssman was, however, a man of advanced thinking and since 1912 had conducted a design and patents office at Johannisthal and maintained a close relationship with various branches of the aircraft industry.

Among other activities he promoted the use of quality plywood produced by Bruening & Sohn AG, the owners of the four largest factories in Germany making this material. This company had the best possible equipment and highly skilled personnel for the production of extremely thin, diagonally bonded, weatherproof veneer plywood. It also produced a heavier grade which contained a thin steel mesh layer. Forssman felt sure that, using the Bruening grades of this material, wings could be built that would have weight and strength advantages over the normal type of construction.

Bruening at that time had no intention of entering the field of aircraft design and construction, wishing to remain as material suppliers to the German aircraft industry. However, Forssman convinced them that they themselves should make wings out of plywood for a large already established aircraft manufacturer, to that manufacturer's specification, using constructional techniques that he had worked out. Forssman's interest in the subject was obviously to increase the turnover for

Bruening & Sohn AG and to receive a percentage of the income that would result from the sale of component wings.

Whether or not Forssman had already approached other aircraft manufacturers before contacting Fokker is not known, but he discussed his ideas on plywood construction with Anthony Fokker in Berlin at the end of March 1916. He was able to offer that Bruening would complete two sets of sample wings, at their own expense and without any obligation, one set to be used in a loading test to destruction (to be witnessed by Fokker) to show the strength of the structure, the other for use on the aeroplane concerned. Fokker also thought that the style of construction described by Forssman would result in an improvement over conventional methods, and agreed that Forssman should contact Martin Kreutzer, the Fokker designer at Schwerin, for the necessary drawings of the wing for the latest Fokker type, that component having just been completed.

The only information that Forssman requested was the exact external measurements of the wings, details of the spar root fittings to the fuselage and those for the bracing wires, as well as the form of the aerofoil sections used. It is significant that Forssman did not ask for the dimensions of the internal parts of the wing, or details of its structure; this indicates that his system must have had its own internal features, and the finished plywood-covered wing would thus only have the same physical shape and size of the wing required. A few days later, Fokker sent wing assembly drawings as well as a blueprint copy of the aerofoil section from the company's Versuchs-Eindecker (experimental monoplane – apparently the M20) and stated that this wing was suitable for the special construction that Forssman had outlined.

When Forssman described his idea of fabricating wings out of plywood to Fokker, it could not have escaped Fokker's attention that the increased strength and resistance to torsion and flexural bending that such structures possessed, might provide a means of pro-

14. Leutnant Werner Voss in the Fokker V 4 triplane at Schwerin, late June/early July 1917. At the time he was acting Staffelfuehrer in Jagdstaffel 14 and had over 30 victories to his credit.

15. The massive dimensions of the double box spars of the lower wing of the modified V 4 are evident here. Equally apparent is the almost flimsy construction of the rear part of the wing, the 1.5mm (1/16in) thick plywood ribs being well perforated with lightening holes and stiffened by cap strips. The plywood leading-edge fitted to the port side reveals that this terminated in a straight line short of the spar on the under surface. The thin wooden strip through the ribs will be supplemented by a length of 1mm steel wire cleated to the rib tails to provide a trailing-edge. The only additional bracing applied before covering consisted of two linen tapes running spanwise and alternating between the tops and bottoms of adjacent ribs to prevent them twisting under the stress of the doped fabric covering.

▲14

16. Fokker liked to use human ballast to demonstrate the strength of his structures, its publicity value in photographs being that there was no doubt about the weight applied. Here 24 Schwerin workmen stand on the double box spars of the centre wing, its span lengthened to provide the increase in wing area for the modified V 4.

▲15   ▼16

ducing wooden wings similar to the all-metal cantilever wings developed by Hugo Junkers, and used on his Junkers J 1 monoplane which first flew on 12 December 1915. Fokker was obviously impressed by the cantilever concept at this time, but it is equally apparent that Forssman's offer to make a wing with plywood for the Fokker M20 was not for a cantilever structure, since his letter to Fokker Flugzeugwerke requesting details of the latest Fokker wing mentions fittings for external bracing wires. He may only have asked for these details since the Fokker M20 wing used them, but it is important to appreciate that one of the features employed by Forssman, even at this early stage, was to utilize the full depth of the aerofoil section as a spar height, and in doing this, bearing in mind the necessity to keep his structures light, he may have used hollow box spars. These were essential in wooden cantilever wing construction, and became a characteristic of the later Fokker thick wing. Thus Forssman may already have had cantilever ideas in mind when he first approached Bruening & Sohn AG with the intention of producing plywood wings; a knowledgeable engineer like Forssman would have been well aware, as undoubtedly Fokker was, of the advantages of such structures.

The Forssman/Bruening wings for the experimental monoplane were apparently not completed, but wings of the same type were made for the single-bay version of the Fokker M17, the basic airframe of the Fokker D II which was already outmoded and thus thought to have been a purely experimental venture into a biplane plywood wing cellule. This work led to wings of similar construction being made for Fokker's latest design, the M22, which was seen as a Fokker D II replacement. This was the aerodynamically clean single-bay biplane already described. The finished plywood wings were some 8 per cent lighter than the normal type of wings without fabric covering. Thus it can be seen that Forssman's original claim that his wings would be lighter than conventional wings was justified; that they were considerably stronger is beyond question. However, the development period of the plywood wings for the M22 had become protracted, and it was not until 12 November 1916 that the plywood wing cellule for this aircraft was sent to the appropriate Idflieg department, Pruefanstalt und Werft (Test Institute and Workshop – PuW) at Adlershof for testing. Doubtless by this time the practicality of using such wings with external bracing had been overtaken by events, and the Fokker emphasis was now on a self-supporting aerodynamically clean lifting surface.

Apart from the obvious incentive provided by Junkers' work, what may have given Fokker the impetus to go for the completely cantilever wing – and be rid of external bracing once and for all – was the revelation that thick aerofoil sections possessed drag properties that were no more deficient, in comparison with the amount of lift generated, than thin aerofoil sections. This is called the lift/drag ratio: it varies, of course, with the angle of attack, but there is a specific relationship between these properties in every aerofoil section. This information, which was circulated to industry, was the result of wind-tunnel measurements made in the summer of 1916 (presumably under Professor Dr L. Prandtl at the University of Goettingen) during an evaluation of aerofoil sections for propeller blades, and was said to have been discovered more or less accidently. Once determined, its application to wing aerofoil sections was investigated, and there can be little doubt that the favourable results obtained launched Fokker into the realm of cantilever wing design.*

Forssman/Bruening were obviously anticipating orders for the superior plywood wings that they had developed for the Fokker M22 (D V), but in the event no production order was given and this aeroplane was manufactured with conventional wings. Fokker's reasons for this (stated in early January 1917) were: the protracted development period, 200 machines of the type already built, and that the D V would be replaced by a new aircraft type (in all probability the V 1, work on which had already commenced). Fokker's exaggeration of D V production (at that time only three Fokker D Vs had been accepted by the military authorities) was obviously to dispel hopes of series production of the plywood wings. This must have been a disappointment for Forssman and whether or not he was enthusiastic about Fokker's statement that the wing experiments then being conducted at Schwerin into both semi-cantilever (braced by a single strut only) and fully cantilever types were suited to the method of construction that he had introduced and developed for Fokker is not known. Forssman was by now engaged in the design and construction of a giant triplane powered by ten engines in tandem, at Bruening's Grossauheim factory near Hanau, which facility had made the afore-mentioned experimental plywood wings, and his degree of involvement in the first Fokker wooden cantilever wing has not been established.

*A systematic comparison of the lift/drag ratios of very thick aerofoil sections had probably not been carried out previously, since the very high drag values of such sections made them less efficient than thinner sections in the externally braced wing structures that had become accepted practice. Junkers, whose cantilever wing ideas went back to 1910, required a thick wing, and after extensive wind-tunnel testing had arrived at his 'Junkers-Profil', but his findings were understandably not widely known at that time outside his own organization.

17. Fokker V 4 (modified). The short-span wings were replaced by new wings of 17½m² area and with aerodynamically balanced ailerons of greater area than those previously used. These features would cause the loss of torsional rigidity to become more pronounced and interplane struts had to be fitted between the wing spars to counter the aileron reaction. Note that an aerodynamically balanced elevator has also been fitted.

▲17

18. Reinhold Platz (on the step-ladder) watches Fokker threading the hemp ammunition belt into its

collecting box during a functioning check on guns and propeller synchronization gear, by running the engine and

firing the guns out into the nearby Schweriner See. This machine, with its burnished aluminium engine cowling, is

thought to be the prototype Fokker V 5 triplane (Works No 1697), designated at this time as F I 101/17.

▼18

19. This is apparently the prototype Fokker V 5 (Works No 1697) being flown at Schwerin before being sent to Adlershof for static load testing as part of the Typenpruefung (type test), a procedure that all German aircraft types underwent to ensure adherence to the requirements laid down in the Idflieg contract with the manufacturer. Despite the painted camouflage finish, the aircraft retains its natural aluminium engine cowling.

20. The Fokker V 6 (Works No 1698) was an attempt to produce a triplane fighter using the 160hp six-cylinder in-line water-cooled Mercedes D III engine. It was heavy (880kg all-up weight), and slow and lacked the manoeuvrability conferred on the lighter Fokker V 5 by the characteristics of the rotary engine. The vertical motor car-type radiator in the fuselage nose was a feature that later Fokker designs would use to advantage.

19▲ 20▼

19

▲21 ▼22

21. Richthofen was present (background) when Fokker (seated in 102/17) conversed with Major-General von Lossberg, Chief of the General Staff of IV Armee, during demonstrations of the first Fokker triplane assigned to Jasta 11 at Marckebeeke aerodrome near Courtrai in August 1917.

22. Anthony Fokker, a keen cine-photographer, is seen at Marckebeeke in August 1917 about to film Manfred von Richthofen preparing for a flight and then taking off in 102/17. Richthofen's flying clothing is shown on the port bottom wing. The camera is in position and the triplane will be pushed ahead and turned to the right through some 90° to place Fokker in its starboard quarter, from which location the filming was done. The results of Fokker's hand-cranking on this occasion are well known and the footage taken continues to be used in almost every film documentary on First World War aviation.

Fokker's interest in cantilever wings doubtless received a boost when on *22 December 1916* he was allowed to fly the Junkers J *2* all-metal cantilever monoplane at Adlershof. In correspondence with Forssman at this time he stated his intention of having Forssman build several sets of experimental wings, 'especially since the torsional stiffness of your wings is very good'. Fokker felt that Forssman's method of fabrication was particularly suited to the type of wings that he had in mind, and he mentioned his experiments with box spars, 'in order to give you the basis of the strength requirement'. Fokker also asked Forssman if he was in a position to supply some 40 square metres of plywood of the same thickness that had been used on the first set of wings (M20 or M17) since the thinner material used on the M22 wings was 'considerably too weak for my present purpose'. This purpose was apparently that of skinning short-span cantilever wings of deep camber.

In creating the wooden cantilever wing there were features that broke completely with traditional types of construction. Hitherto wings had used spindled I-section spars and employed simple lattice ribs of thin wooden strips. Resistance to distortion caused by centre of pressure movement and the twisting effect of the ailerons was provided by external bracing wires; these wires had large purchase angles for bracing the usual biplane wing cellule into a structure which, when considered as a whole, was cantilever. Designers were well aware of the large amount of drag produced by the many struts and wires used to brace their wings, but the thin aerofoil sections then in use did not allow the wings themselves to be made strong enough to dispense with the external bracing.

To resist bending, any structure must have depth, and once Fokker realized that thick aerofoils were practical, and knowing that deeper more efficient spars could be used, he caused his box spars to be made with increased cross-sectional area. These had plywood sides with heavier wooden tops and bottoms called webs and booms or flanges, respectively. The greater part of the material was concentrated near the upper and lower wing surfaces where it did the most good in resisting bending; in addition, a box section is more resistant to twisting than is a narrower solid spar of the same weight. Two spars could resist torsion individually, but more strength than that was needed, and plain plywood ribs were used, stiffened by thin wooden flanges. This divided the wing into a series of cells or boxes, each capable of resisting torsion and thus bracing the wing internally. When this structure was completely covered with plywood, the covering was made to share the work of the spar flanges, and so was born the stressed-skin wing, which in later years, when made of metal, would be almost universally employed in aircraft construction.

The Forssman system of construction was adopted and modified by Fokker, who on occasion used fabric instead of plywood as a wing covering. The basic concept was used on all his subsequent First World War aircraft, which were later identified by the Fokker Flugzeugwerke designation of 'V' for Verspannungslos, meaning without external bracing – i.e., cantilever.†

†The 'V' designations were introduced in July 1917 and were applied retrospectively to earlier aircraft types. To prevent confusion they are used in this book to identify Fokker V 1–V 6, although at the time these aircraft used Roman numerals prefixed by the letter 'D' in an earlier Fokker company designation system, which was, of course, discontinued with the adoption of the 'V' numbers.

FOKKER V 1 – V 3

DURING the early months of 1917 Fokker was no longer a supplier of effective front-line fighters. However, as production of the Fokker D V proceeded, interesting events were taking place in the Versuchsabteilung (experimental section) at Schwerin where a single-seater of unusual appearance was under construction. The forward fuselage of this aeroplane bore a certain resemblance to that of the Fokker D V, but the circular engine cowling had a tapered chord which was necessary for it to blend into the abnormally large circular cross-section of the well-conceived fuselage of fine streamlined form, which was stringered over its whole length, terminating in a point at the rear.

The most unusual feature was the thick-section, plywood-covered wings, completely devoid of any bracing struts or wires. As already described, this was possible since spars having sufficient vertical depth to give the necessary strength meant that a deep, highly cambered aerofoil section had to be used. This form of construction was the outcome of the Forssman work already mentioned, but who actually designed and did the stressing of this first wooden cantilever biplane's wings has yet to be determined. Reinhold Platz, the

23. Voss's mechanics, Gefreiter (lance-corporal) Rueser and Flieger (private) Karl Timm, with 103/17 at Marcke aerodrome near Courtrai shortly after the arrival of this aircraft in August 1917. Note the lack of wingtip skids, one of the features by which Fokker V 4 triplanes can be identified.

▲ 23

24. Leutnant Werner Voss, Staffelfuehrer of Jasta 10, with Fokker F I 103/17. The engine cowling was painted chrome yellow, the identifying colour of Jasta 10, and its shape with the two holes for the entry of cooling air obviously lent itself

▼ 24

to the application of the white facial features. These are based on the fierce warrior faces painted on Japanese kites. (See notes on Triplane Markings, Appendix IX).

25. German soldiers with the wreckage of Oberleutnant Kurt Wolff's 102/17 near the village of Nachtigall, north of Wervicq, after he had been shot down and killed on 15

▼ 25

September 1917. The apparent lack of fire damage contradicts some previously published accounts that Wolff was shot down in flames.

welding expert, who was in charge of the Versuchs-abteilung – which workshop was tasked with making and testing parts to the drawings produced in the design office of the engineering department – has related that the reason for the appearance of this machine, which was retrospectively designated V 1, was that 'Fokker was particularly interested in proving the practicality of cantilever wings, which were not regarded as "safe" '. Bearing in mind recent experiences of the structural weaknesses that had permeated previous Fokker designs, an excess of strength was a good 'fault' for the engineering department designers to incorporate into such a structure, and this might explain the massive proportions of the upper mainplane; refinement could come later.

The top wing was pivoted about the front spar, hinged at the apices of two tripods of centre-section struts, and its angle of incidence could be varied in flight between $-1°$ and $+7°$ by means of a small hand crank. The lower wing, of much smaller area, was installed at a fixed angle. Both wings were tapered in front elevation and in plan, the latter being obtained by sweeping back the leading edges, and this gave an even distribution of load over their surfaces. The 'all-flying' rudder and elevator had long been used on Fokker designs, but now this very sensitive type of flying control surface was extended to the wings to give movement in the rolling plane by pivoting the wingtips. All these control surfaces were aerodynamically balanced by being hinged approximately one-third of their chord aft of their leading edges, and were actuated from within the surface themselves, further eliminating parasitic drag due to the absence of operating horns and cables in the airflow.

The undercarriage axle was faired with an aerofoil-shaped wing which not only removed the parasitic drag of the axle but provided sufficient lift to equal the weight of the entire undercarriage. In performing this function, the efficiency of its low aspect-ratio rectangular shape was improved by the 'end-plate' effect of the fabric-covered wire-spoked wheels. This was a feature that Fokker would retain on his subsequent production designs, such as the Dr I, D VI, D VII and E V (D VIII).

The engine used was the 110hp Le Rhône, the first time such an engine had been used on a Fokker design. It was probably a captured example, since at that time Oberursel had not finalized their preparations for the production of their copy of this engine (Oberursel UR II). As early as the beginning of March 1916 Idflieg had been asked by the General Staff (doubtless at Major Siegert's instigation) to copy the nine-cylinder 110hp Le Rhône which, with its pushrod-operated inlet valves, was far superior to engines of the Gnome type with their automatic piston valves. However, it was not until December that Oberursel were ready to deliver engines, and the Oberursel UR II did not pass its Idflieg acceptance test until March 1917. In the interim engines were being manufactured and it is also possible that Fokker was given a pre-acceptance engine for test purposes. Official documentation often calls the Oberursel UR II a Le Rhône; thus the nomenclature alone does not positively identify the origin of the engine.

In the design of the aircraft certain known aerodynamic principles were maintained. To reduce biplane interference, a sesquiplane layout was adopted. Further, as the incidence of the top wing could be varied in flight, it was essential to ensure that the changes in lift and drag that this would incur were a direct result of the incidence changes; and to augment the protection afforded by the sesquiplane layout, a larger gap than normal was used between the wings. To prevent biplane interference completely, the gap has to be approximately four times the wing chord; thus the wide chord of the top wing may have dictated the larger than normal gap used. It was necessary to fill the large gap with fuselage and not drag-creating struts, which possibly accounts for the depth of this component. Also, the best known streamline shape was one of circular cross-section having a fineness ratio of approximately four, with the maximum width approximately one-third of the total length aft from the nose. These criteria are present in this fuselage; i.e., it has the optimum shape for least resistance.

The 110hp Le Rhône, which weighed 148kg, was of similar diameter to the Oberursel U I, but because of the large cross-sectional area of the fuselage, the cowling had to be of tapered form. The relatively small diameter engine gave a low frontal area and the fitting of a large spun aluminium spinner over the propeller boss ensured that the nose was well streamlined. As on the Fokker D V, the spinner performed another important function: it deflected and accelerated the airflow into a small annular space opposite the engine cylinders and improved cooling. In addition, the use of a tapered-chord cowling resulted in its periphery acquiring an aerofoil section shape that conferred low drag properties upon this component.*

From the foregoing, it can be seen that the V 1 was not merely a vehicle with which to fly the first Fokker wooden cantilever wing. This design was an essay to the very limits of knowledge to find an aerodynamically clean aeroplane. Many of the features showed advanced thinking and illustrate how thoroughly the problem of

*It is significant that such cowling refinements were not generally appreciated until the advent of Townend rings and NACA cowlings, introduced many years later as a result of extensive wind tunnel testing.

26. This Fokker photograph showing Leutnant Werner Voss seated in a production Fokker V 5 triplane, which has been fitted with improved crash pad protection around the gun butts and with a temporary headrest, confirms that Voss was at Schwerin during September 1917.

27. The first Fokker Dr I to be dispatched from Schwerin to the front was 115/17 (Works No 1783) on 4 October. Seen shortly after its arrival at La Neuville, the aircraft was assigned to Leutnant Heinrich Gontermann, Staffelfuehrer of Jasta 15. Apparently it was intended to introduce the type into VII Armee in anticipation of forming JG II in that area. Gontermann died from injuries received when this machine crashed due to structural failure of the upper mainplane on 30 October.

▲26   ▼27

drag reduction was treated. This effort was rewarded by an extremely good climbing performance, an important quality in a fighter. Total all-up weight was 563kg, wing area was $17m^2$ and a speed of 180km/hr was achieved, while the elapsed times to climb to the heights stated were (approximately): 1,000m in 2½min; 2,000m in 6min; 3,000m in 11min; 4,000m in 19min; and 5,000m in 30min.

To underline how outstanding this performance was for early 1917, one has only to reflect on the climbing ability of the Albatros D III, which was the best German fighter in the spring of 1917. Although factory-new examples were reportedly capable of climbing to 5,000 metres in 25 minutes, after a period of use with the front-line units aircraft of this type possessed lesser perform-ance. Operational examples of both the Albatros D III and the later Albatros D V were in fact only able to climb to a height of some 3,600 metres in 30 minutes.[†]

Fokker was very enthusiastic about the V 1 and stated in his 1931 biography *Flying Dutchman* that: 'Perfection was my sole consideration . . . More modern than any plane produced during the war by either side, it looked good, an almost sure test of a fine airplane . . . Taking it up in the air, I found the biplane so fast, sensitive and altogether satisfactory that I felt certain of having designed a plane which would be immediately accepted and rushed to the front. It had both speed and climb, and went through all combat manoeuvres like greased lightning.'

However, for reasons unknown, the military authori-ties did not award Fokker a production contract for this outstanding aeroplane. Whether the memory of Fokker structural shortcomings was too recent, or whether Idflieg, who supported the Junkers all-metal cantilever wing programme, felt that the concept of equivalent wooden structures should first prove themselves further, is not known; but an apparently disenterested Idflieg left Fokker to his own devices. The Fokker V 1 obviously had development potential. By deleting the bottom wing and refining the upper wing, a parasol rotary-engined fighter could have been produced some eighteen months before it actually was, when the Fokker E V emerged in August 1918.

There was, however, a basic problem which may have been the deciding factor – the shortage of a suitable engine. Oberursel production of their UR II was beset with difficulties, mainly those related to the shortage of castor lubricating oil. Although 1,200 tons of a first pressing of this commodity had been found in Antwerp docks during the occupation of Belgium in 1914, and immediately reserved for rotary engine lubrication, it had by this time mostly been used up in supplementing the limited home supply. Because stocks were barely sufficient for front-line use, Oberursel experimented with a system in which the engine was started up using castor oil and then switched to mineral oil, but this was unsuccessful and led to engine seizures. Despite using aluminium pistons in the UR II, there was an urgent need for an ersatz rotary-engine lubricating oil. This was developed – known as T 50, it was 50 per cent Voltol (fish and rape seed oil) and 50 per cent mineral oil – but the engine had to be modified to use it and did not pass its acceptance test with this oil (Bauartenpruefung) until August.[*]

Fokker, in pursuit of his policy of exploring the relative merits of stationary and rotary engines in his designs, had, immediately after the completion of the V 1, taken steps to produce a 160hp Mercedes-powered version of his radical biplane. Film, presumably taken personally by Fokker, who was a keen cinephoto-grapher, shows that when the V 1 was returned to the Versuchsabteilung for modifications found necessary after flight testing, work on the V 2 was well advanced. The modifications to the V 1 included the fitting of a new vertical tail surface – a faired fin was introduced, raising the rudder – and the reduction of the angle of incidence of the bottom wing, which features were already embodied on the V 2. Although the variable-incidence gear was retained for the upper wing of the V 2, this component had an aerofoil section of much greater camber than that used on the V 1. This was doubtless required since the V 2 was a heavier aircraft; its engine plus the necessary radiator, which was of Windhoff manufacture, weighed almost twice as much as the Le Rhône. In the film footage mentioned, the appearance of the V 2 wing actually being built in the same shop indicates that Fokker Flugzeugwerke were now making this specialized construction themselves, without recourse to Forssman/Bruening facilities. Despite Fokker records stating that the reason for building the 160hp Mercedes-powered version was to obtain better climbing performance, the availability of engines may have been the real reason for its appear-ance. In the event, the performance of the V 2 was considerably below that of the V 1.

In an attempt to lessen this deficiency, modified

[†]On 7 June 1917 Leutnant Ernst Udet of Jagdstaffel 15 compared the climbing performances of both the Albatros D III and the Albatros D V. Although the D III reached 4,400 metres in 45 minutes and the D V achieved 4,700 metres in 54 minutes, both aircraft reached 3,600 metres in 30 minutes. (Document from Walter Behrend, Udet's mechanic in Jasta 15.)

[*]Castor oil was obtained from the seeds of the Ricinus communis plant which were bruised between rollers, poured into hempen bags and pressed. The plant was a native of Africa and was grown elsewhere, but required a hot climate, which explains Germany's limited home supply.

28. Some of the first triplanes delivered to Jasta 11 had what appears to have been aluminium-coloured engine cowlings. From the stencilled number under the top wing centre-section, this is 104/17 (Works No 1772), which was accepted on 13 September at Schwerin and was one of the initial batch of six triplanes for Jasta 11 dispatched on 10 October. It is seen at Varsenaere aerodrome near Brugge, where its unusual configuration is a source of interest to the Jasta 28 personnel in the picture.

▲ 28

29. Five triplanes of Jasta 11 at Wasquehal aerodrome near Lille, late October 1917, during a visit to Jasta 17, possibly during a flight to familiarize units in the neighbouring VI Armee area with the triplane's appearance. It is not known whether the aluminium-coloured engine cowlings on the nearest two triplanes were painted silver or were left in their natural finish, but the usual 'engine-turning' applied to aluminium components to resist corrosion cannot be discerned in this photograph. Although the triplane in the background has a dark engine cowling, it is possible that some early triplanes left Schwerin with unpainted engine cowlings; however, that shown may have been a painted marking used at this time to aid identification and prevent possible confusion with the Sopwith Triplane.

▲ 29   ▼ 30

30. The arrival of the Fokker triplanes at the front, and their similar appearance to the Sopwith Triplane, caused confusion between friend and foe alike. The standard of aircraft identification was not high on either side and recognition was usually made by noting the other machine's national insignia. On 29 October 1917 Vizefeldwebel (acting Sergeant-Major) Josef Lautenschlager of Jasta 11 was shot down and killed north of

Houthulst Forest while flying 113/17 (Works No 1781) by a Vizefeldwebel pilot of another Jagdstaffel in IV Armee. The pilot was to have been court-martialled, but Richthofen ascertained that the use of his triplanes had not been promulgated widely enough within the IV Armee area and was able to prove that the unfortunate pilot's unit had not been informed. The blame, Richthofen maintained, rested with the inefficiency of the Kogenluft-Nachrichtenwesen (intelligence/communications service). He went further than merely obtaining the reprieve of the pilot, but arranged for his transfer to JG I, where he became a successful fighter pilot, but his identity was never revealed.

thinking produced the V 3. A conventional tail unit was fitted and the adjustable top wing incidence gear discarded. The wing gap seems to have been increased over that of the V 2, and since Fokker records state that the height of both the V 1 and the V 2 was the same, the length of the undercarriage must have been shortened, although this is not obvious from photographs. It is assumed that the V 2 and the V 3 were in fact the same basic aircraft, and that an increase in wing area to $22m^2$ was effected on the V 2 and this was retained on the V 3. In the experimental work done at Schwerin there is no doubt that wing interchange took place, and that several wings of varying aerofoil sections were tried.

Despite a marginal increase in weight, repeated test climbs eventually showed an improvement on the V 2's performance, but the figures for the V 1 climbs could not be reached, far less bettered. The lesser climbing performances of the V 2 and V 3 were undoubtedly due to the heavier all-up weights of these machines (921kg and 938kg respectively), despite the use of 160hp. In the 30-minute elapsed climbing time that was used above as a comparison for the relative climbing performances of the V 1 and the Albatros D III/D V, the V 2 climbed to 4,100 metres and the V 3 to 4,400 metres. Both were therefore better performers in this respect than operational examples of the Albatros types mentioned. One would have expected that the final version of this aeroplane at least would have been further investigated by Idflieg, but once again no official interest appears to have been shown. The good performances were due, in part, to the advanced fuselage design, and it was realized that the deletion of this feature on production aircraft due to labour and cost considerations would degrade the performance. However, the saving in weight would have been beneficial and it is considered that the resulting performance would still have been appreciably better than that enjoyed by the Albatros types mentioned.

Manfred von Richthofen writing to the Kogenluft technical officer, Oberleutnant von Falkenhayn, on 18 July 1917 from hospital in Courtrai – where he was recovering from a serious wound in the head sustained in air combat on 6 July – had several pertinent things to say about fighter aeroplanes. He could afford to be frank with his correspondent since they were close friends. The letter is a highly revealing document and contains two references that tend to support the existence of Idflieg bias against Fokker, as has already been suggested. The first is hinted at in a general statement, after Richthofen bemoans the inferiority of the Albatros D V:

'Even if companies have been unreliable in the past and have behaved in an irresponsible manner, we must use them and give them our support when they produce a type that is even only slightly better than this damned Albatros. As long as the Albatros company does not have energetic competition, we will be stuck with our Albatros D III (D V).' There is no doubt that Richthofen is referring to Fokker, but now he becomes more specific and only four lines later writes:

'What is, for example, happening to Fokker? He has two machines which are superior to the Albatros, but they are not in production. There is his cantilever biplane with the stationary engine. It is without question, faster and possesses better turning qualities than the Albatros D V, but, in spite of this, is not being built. I believe Schwarzenberger is behind this.'*

The other Fokker machine referred to by Richthofen was a triplane design which was '. . . no longer in the development stage, but which has already demonstrated an excellent climbing and speed performance, which we must now definitely support and send to the front in large numbers as soon as we have rotary engines.'

However, unknown to Richthofen, an order had already been placed for 20 Fokker triplanes on 14 July. This active creation of triplane production by Idflieg was the result of a decision taken at the time Richthofen lay ill in hospital. It is thus not to be wondered at that he was unaware of it when he dictated his letter of 18 July. As already stated, the triplane's existence was known to him and also, of course, the acute shortage of powerplants for it – this situation pertained before he was wounded. The triplane that he knew about was the Fokker V 4, doubtless having been briefed on the properties of this forerunner of the Fokker Dr I by Leutnant Werner Voss, who had already flown the machine at Schwerin.

*Hauptmann Kurt Schwarzenberger of Idflieg, an officer responsible for the technical development of fighter aircraft.

▲31

▲32

31. Gontermann, his face smeared with Frostsalbe (chilblain ointment) as a safeguard against frostbite, in 115/17, shortly before his last flight. The high rear-mounted windscreen was not a standard fitting and probably restricted access to the left-hand gun's bolt lever and ammunition feed. The prominent whorl in the fuselage fabric immediately below the cockpit should be noted; the aircraft was then only a few weeks old. Such whorls were caused by poor quality dope and exposed the bare fabric, robbing it locally of weatherproofing.

32. Gontermann in 115/17 about to take off from La Neuville, watched by his mechanic. Annotations in Leutnant Arnzten's photograph album, from which this and the previous photograph originated, indicate that this was the fatal flight on 30 October.

▼33

▼34

33. Wreckage of 115/17 showing that all the wing ribs had broken away from the box spar. The report made by Leutnant Arnzten, the Jasta 15 Technical Officer, stated that the right-hand aileron came off in the air; the ZAK Sturzkommission (crash investigators) maintained that the left aileron was the first component to detach. As can be seen, the left-hand aileron is still attached to its operating cables, thus the actual term used by ZAK of 'weggeflattert' (fluttered away) is a misnomer. Furthermore, its condition does not correspond with Arntzen's damage description of the detached aileron (see Appendix I).

34. In the original photograph of Gontermann's wrecked triplane, both aileron cables on the left-hand side, on the rear face of the spar, can be seen to be intact, thus providing further proof that the left-hand aileron did not completely detach in the air as ZAK stated. This is one of several discrepancies between Leutnant Arntzen's eyewitness account and the official report submitted by the crash commission included in the Appendix.

FOKKER V 4 – V 5 TRIPLANES

IT would appear that at the beginning of June 1917 Fokker became aware that Idflieg was about to award Probeauftraege (test contracts) of three triplanes each to certain manufacturers in order to evaluate by practical means the merits of fighters of this configuration. They were obviously moved to take this action because of the reported superiority of the British Sopwith Triplane over the German fighters then in use, and indeed such contracts were issued to both Siemens-Schuckert-Werke and Pfalz-Flugzeugwerke that month. However, during the intervening period Fokker had adapted his cantilever wing structure to suit the fuselage of a biplane demonstrator that he had under construction for Austria–Hungary, and he quickly produced a triplane fighter known as the Fokker V 4. Despite the rapidity of its creation, this was an aircraft whose performance surpassed even that which had been obtained with the revolutionary V 1.

The natural benefit of the triplane over the biplane of the same wing area is that the individual wings can be made of shorter span; consequently wing structures of lesser weight still possess the high strength required. The cantilever wing cellule was therefore used to advantage in this machine. In addition, by covering the wings of the V 4 with fabric instead of plywood, which had been used previously on Fokker cantilever wing designs, even more weight was saved. Dispensing with the plywood covering was a bold stroke, since it removed some of the strength of the structure, and this would have its repercussions. However, the use of a torsion box, whereby the two box spars were coupled close together into a very strong single spar, was thought to be sufficient to take care of both the flexural and the torsional loads on the short span triplane's wings. The plywood-covered leading-edge came within an ace of creating the D-section torsion box of later years, but the leading-edge plywood did not contribute greatly to the strength of the wing since it terminated short of the spar on the lower surface and was serrated on the upper surface, being merely attached by its apices to the spar between the ribs; thus its function was one of fairing, rather than strength. In the event, the double box spar was sufficiently strong on its own and there are no cases on record where this component ever failed in flight.

The simplified steel tube fuselage structure used on the V 4, with flat keel surfaces, gave better stability in flight than the round section of the streamlined fuselages of the V 1 – V 3 types. As already stated, it also saved weight and, as in the case of the fabric-covered wings, was easier and much more economical to produce.

This aircraft, powered by the 110hp Le Rhône, weighed 528kg, had a wing area of $14m^2$ and achieved a speed of 200km/hr with the following (approximate) climbing performance: 1,000m in 2½min; 2,000m in 5½min; 3,000m in 10min; 4,000m in 17min; and 5,000m in 28min.

These data, however presented, must have caused Hauptmann Schwarzenberger and other officials of Idflieg to sit up and take notice of the experimental 'goings-on' at Schwerin. The existence of this machine was reported to Allied Intelligence who gave details of it in a report dated 2 July 1917. Thus, it is reasonable to assume that the Fokker V 4 was flying from approximately 25 June. But whether or not Fokker was now given a similar contract to that of Siemens and Pfalz because of this enterprise – a phenomenal achievement in terms of elapsed time – or was awarded the contract on the strength of his V 1 – V 3 experimental work, is not known. The fact remains that at the beginning of July he received a Probeauftrag for three Vierdeckern (quadruplanes). The nomenclature is not as strange as it appears, since at this time both Fokker and Idflieg considered the aerofoil-section-shaped undercarriage axle fairing of the Fokker types as a wing.

Later in July Idflieg further reported that Fokker had under construction three new fighter types (Vierdeckern) for different engines. These were obviously the aircraft from the Probeauftrag granted a short time previously. It is considered that the first of these was the V 4. Fokker, who possessed an uncanny ability to perceive the changes that were required for better performance and handling in his designs, caused the basic airframe to be modified by fitting greater-span wings with increased wing area and aerodynamically balanced control surfaces. These alterations to the wing cellule, especially the more effective ailerons, highlighted insufficient wing torsional rigidity and made the fitting of interplane struts between the spars a necessity to increase this. It was this major modification work that caused the V 4 to be classed as being 'under construction' in the Idflieg report. Being an astute businessman, Fokker, by including the V 4 in his list of triplane prototypes to meet the Idflieg contract, thus recouped his development expenditure, although this machine was destined for

▲35

35. The wreckage of Leutnant Guenther Pastor's triplane, 121/17 (Works No 1832), which crashed 1km north of Moorseele on 31 October 1917. There are no details of the nature of any manoeuvres undertaken before the aircraft, apparently descending in a normal gliding attitude, suffered structural failure of the top mainplane, which resulted in the fatal crash. This machine had been on the strength of Jasta 11 for only a few days and its loss, as well as that of 115/17 of Jasta 15 caused the structural integrity of the design to be investigated (see Appendix I). Note that despite the aircraft's short life, the white backgrounds of the national insignia (including, incorrectly, that on the rudder) have been painted out to leave the regulation 5cm-wide white borders. From what can be seen of the engine cowling, this appears to be natural aluminium, possibly left unpainted for the reason already mentioned.

36. Another view of Pastor's crash. Note that the aileron pulleys and their bracket on the rear web of the box spar just inboard of the interplane strut are still intact (see Appendix I).

▼36

Austria–Hungary. The identities of the other two prototype triplanes are known from Fokker records and were undoubtedly the V 5 and the V 6. Tabulating this information gives the following:

Fokker designation	Works number	Engine	Date commenced
D VI (later V 4)	1661	110hp Le Rhône	? July (modification only)
D VI (later V 5)	1697	110hp UR II	5 July
D VII (later V 6)	1698	160hp Mercedes	7 July

Despite lack of official encouragement, Fokker had produced outstanding performances from his V 1, V 3 and V 4 designs, and the performance of the modified V 4 was now improved to such an extent that Idflieg could not fail to be impressed. This machine, powered by the 110hp Le Rhône, now had a wing area of $18.6m^2$, an all-up weight of 571kg and a speed that is variously reported in Fokker documentation as 200km/hr and 'not less than 180km/hr'. Climbing performance (times are approximate) was: 1,000m in 1½min; 2,000m in 4½min; 3,000m in 8½min; 4,000m in 14min; and 5,000m in 18min.

If these statistics alone did not change Idflieg's attitude towards Fokker and his designs, no doubt the flying demonstration that Fokker put on before the military acceptance commission did. The exceptional manoeuvrability, especially in the rolling plane due to the triplane's short wingspan, coupled with the gyroscopic effect of the rotary engine, as well as the speed and rate of climb of this light aerodynamically clean design, were exploited to the full in Fokker's skilled hands. He had flown like this before with the V 1 and been ignored. Now he must have demonstrated that triplane to its very limit, and in a manner that only Fokker knew how. The Idflieg bias (there is no other word for it) against the Dutchman now changed to one of unbridled praise and they had to admit that Fokker's triplane was 'erstklassig' (first-class).

On 11 July work began on two pre-production triplanes for front-line evaluation, based on the modified V 4. These were Fokker F I 102/17 (Works No 1729) and F I 103/17 (Works No 1730); and this explains why contemporary Fokker records identify them as Fokker V 4 triplanes. There seems no doubt that the modified V 4 was the aircraft that caused Idflieg to award Fokker a production contract for '20 Fokker III Decker' on 14 July, since the Idflieg report commenting on the fact that the Fokker triplane was the first usable machine of the type, stated that it had reached a height of 5,000 metres in 18 minutes. This performance was retrospectively given in Fokker records as that for the Fokker V 5, and photographs of the modified V 4 were also retrospectively so identified. They were of course, to all intents and purposes, the same aeroplane; both used the same early company designation of D VI, and possessed only detail differences, but the change of designation mentioned has been a source of confusion among researchers for many years. The modified V 4 (works number 1661), which had played such an important part in the birth of the Fokker triplane, left the Schwerin scene in late August, being sent to Mátyásföld near Budapest in Hungary. The first V 5 (works number 1697), now bearing its military designation of Fokker F I 101/17, was a refined version of the modified V 4 and was the true prototype of the Fokker Dr I. This machine was dispatched to Adlershof on 7 August for structural strength tests, which it passed with relatively minor shortcomings.

There was obviously some difficulty with the allocation of a suitable military designation for aircraft of the fighter triplane class. Mention is made in official Idflieg documents in June and July of '3 Decker' and 'III Decker' and the first Fokker triplanes were known as 'F' types, probably only because in the German military aeroplane classification system 'F' had not previously been used. The triplane was a Dreidecker, and it was an abbreviation of this word that was eventually used. When Fokker F I 101/17 passed its Bruchprobe at Adlershof on 11 August, it was called a Fokker Dr I, but an explanation was added to this written use of the new term to clarify its pronunciation – 'spricht: Fokker dre I'. On 19 August this designation was promulgated by Idflieg stating that it was now in use. As a matter of interest, this official document (Flugzeugmeisterei Abt AB Nr 357701) gave the designation as DR, and it was this form that was used in painting the type designation on the aeroplane.

37. Oberleutnant Karl Bodenschatz, Adjutant of JG I, in front of 150/17 (Works No 1862) at Avesnes-le-Sec shortly after this aircraft's arrival in late December 1917. The weather at the time was overcast and foggy and snow had fallen on 28 December.

38. Fokker Dr I 146/17 (Works No 1858) was acceptance-flown at Schwerin on 30 October 1917 and was one of a ten-machine batch dispatched on 12 December for Jasta 11. It is seen at Avesnes-le-Sec shortly after its arrival. Apart from a (possibly) red engine cowling and red wheel covers, the aircraft is in standard factory finish. It was one of a number of triplanes fitted with asymmetrical ailerons in, it is thought, an attempt to improve manoeuvrability in the rolling plane.

39. Seven pilots of Jasta 11 at Avesnes-le-Sec, late December 1917, standing in front of Fokker Dr I 145/17 (Works No 1857), which was another of the triplanes fitted with asymmetrical ailerons. The difference in the pilots' flying attire is noteworthy, as is the use of facemasks to reduce the risk of frostbite. Left to right: Leutnants Schoenebeck, Stapenhorst, Just, Oberleutnant von Boddien, Leutnants von der Osten, Wolff and Steinhaeuser.

40. Jasta Boelcke received its first Fokker D V for the rotary-engine conversion of its pilots on 1 January 1918 in anticipation of receiving triplanes. The pilot is Vizefeldwebel Paul Baeumer, seen here in the snow at Boistrancourt visiting his friend Leutnant von Hippel of Jasta 5, whose green-tailed, white-banded Albatros D V, marked with the initial 'H' on its wing under surfaces, is in the background.

▲ 37   ▼ 38

41. Leutnant Eberhard Stapenhorst's triplane 144/17 (Works No 1856) was lost on 13 January 1918 in what was probably the first successful combat use of the Fokker Dr I, when Leutnant Steinhaeuser was credited with the destruction of an observation balloon at Heudecourt. Stapenhorst's machine was hit by ground fire and forced to land behind British lines; it became the subject of a detailed examination that eventually appeared in the aeronautical press. This triplane was from the 12 December consignment from Schwerin and the reduced area of the starboard aileron is obvious in this unusual view.

▲41

42. Jasta 11 triplane 154/17 (Works No 1866) on Retheuil-Ferme aerodrome near Bohain while visiting Jasta 17 in January 1918. This machine is

▼42

fitted with two small-area ailerons that have had the size of their original aerodynamic

balances reduced. It is one of the batch of fifteen triplanes dispatched from Schwerin on

12/13 December for Jasta 11 and fitted with different types of aileron.

FIRST OPERATIONAL
FOKKER TRIPLANES

THE Zentral-Abnahme-Kommission (Central Acceptance Commission – ZAK) was the Idflieg department for ensuring that laid-down standards of construction were reached during manufacture, acceptance of the aircraft into military service and related matters. These functions were carried out by ZAK regional offices, named Bauaufsichten (BA), located at the aircraft factories.

The output from the Fokker Flugzeugwerke was supervised by BA 13 at Schwerin, and when an aircraft was completed, personnel of this office subjected it to an examination defined by ZAK to verify its completeness and its suitability for military use. This involved test-flying by one of the manufacturer's test pilots (ZAK test pilots were used initially), climbing performance data being recorded by a barograph. Once the aircraft met the laid-down standards, an Abnahmeverhandlung (acceptance contract) was raised and was signed by representatives of both Fokker and BA 13. This contract provided specific details of the aircraft as regards its acceptance flight, and contained data on actual weight, achieved speed, length of take-off and landing runs, tabulated climbing performance of height gained against elapsed time (taken from the barogram, a copy of which was attached to the contract form), type and serial numbers of engine, propeller, machine-guns and all instruments fitted, plus the date of acceptance. The latter was stamped on a metal manufacturer's plate which was riveted to the starboard side of the engine cowling of the triplane, and this plate was also annotated with the works serial number and the manufacturer's aircraft type designation.*

The machine was now government property and the BA office received details concerning its disposition. This dispatch advice stated to which Armee Flug Park (AFP) – the aviation distribution centre for all personnel and equipment within an Army area – the aircraft should be sent. If, exceptionally, the aircraft was to be sent to a storage depot in order not to congest the AFP with prolonged storage – a procedure adopted if it was required to harbour an aircraft type until sufficient numbers were available, before introducing them

simultaneously to the front – it was usually sent to Flieger Lager West at Aachen, the main aviation storage centre for the Western Front.

Military personnel dismantled and loaded the aircraft for shipment by rail. Apart from covering the engine, machine-guns and the cockpit area with greaseproof paper or small waterproof sheets, en route protection was by a heavy tarpaulin cover placed over the complete machine, which had wheels, propeller and wings removed. The aircraft now came under the care of a Begleitkommando (military escort) which would accompany the loaded wagons to their destination. The provision of a Begleitkommando was necessary to prevent any attempt at sabotage and to supervise the handling given by railway personnel, who, not appreciative of the frailty of the cargo entrusted to their care, were responsible for much damage to aeroplanes in transit. In addition, the Begleitkommando kept a close watch on the tarpaulin covers, ensuring that these did not work loose and cause damage by flapping against the aircraft structure or allowing weather to affect airframe components. The military escort's presence also prevented the theft of the tarpaulins by troops and civilians, both at home and in the front areas, who saw them as most desireable items; the worsening economic situation in Germany meant that they were almost irreplaceable.

When the shipment arrived at the appropriate AFP, aircraft were unloaded and assembled by that unit's personnel and held in store until the final recipients were known. Aircraft allocation was decided by the Kommandeur der Flieger (the Staff Officer in charge of all the flying units assigned to an Army – Kofl). Jagdstaffeln then sent pilots to the AFP to collect their machines, and so eventually the aeroplanes came on the strength of the front-line formations.

From the foregoing it can be seen that the manufacturer did not know exactly where his products went. This was deliberate and essential in the interests of security, but in the case of the early shipments of Fokker triplanes, Fokker obviously knew that they were destined for Richthofen's recently formed Jagdgeschwader I (JG I) comprising Jagdstaffeln 4, 6, 10 and 11. Thus there was no need to adhere to the standard routine and, in any case, Idflieg could make exceptions to their normal delivery procedures. In this respect,

*The manufacturer's type designation ceased to be marked on this plate from the effective date of the 1918 BLV.

43. Fokker Dr I 212/17 (Works No 1931) secured to the floor of a flat railway wagon. Later its wings will be packed alongside and vertical supports fitted (as on the following wagon) before being covered by a heavy tarpaulin sheet for en route weather protection during its delivery journey from the factory to the front. This aircraft was one of a four-triplane consignment dispatched from Schwerin on 12 January 1918 for AFP IV. Others in the batch were 204/17, 213/17 and 214/17, all of which were allocated to Jasta Boelcke based at Bavichove near Courtrai in Flanders.

▲ 43

44. This triplane is believed to be 212/17 although its works number cannot be positively deciphered in this photograph. It is known to have been flown by Leutnant Karl Gallwitz, seen (second from left) with his mechanics at Bavichove. The black engine cowling with its white face was part of the Jasta Boelcke unit marking used on the triplane. Note the black and white streamers attached to the wingtip skids.

▲ 44   ▼ 45

45. Factory-fresh 213/17 (Works No 1932) seen on arrival at AFP IV after assembly and before being ferried to Bavichove. It was later flown by Leutnant Fritz Kempf who applied a flamboyant decoration to the machine, but failed to obtain any victories on it.

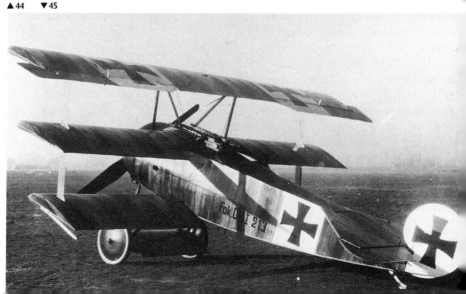

especially with Fokker F I 102/17 and 103/17, these machines were probably sent directly to JG I at Marckebeeke near Courtrai in occupied Belgium, and no doubt Fokker mechanics accompanied the Begleit-kommando.

Both the Fokker V 4 triplanes were accepted by ZAK on 16 August and were dispatched from Schwerin on 21 August. There must have been considerable excitement when these aeroplanes reached their destination. The pilots had been forewarned by Richthofen that they would be receiving the new Fokker triplane, since when he visited his unit from hospital on 20 July, as he was looking over their patched and oft-repaired machines on the aerodrome, he had told them so, adding, as if to bolster the morale of the men sentenced to fly the poorly performing Albatros D V, that the triplanes 'climb like monkeys and are manoeuvrable as the devil'.

The two V 4 triplanes were allocated* to Jasta 11 (102/17) to be flown by Richthofen and the Staffelfuehrer (Jagdstaffel leader or CO) Leutnant Kurt Wolff, and Jasta 10 (103/17) to be flown by the Staffelfuehrer Leutnant Werner Voss. Depite wet and stormy weather, Voss first flew 103/17 during the evening of 28 August, and it is assumed that 102/17 was also test-flown at this time. Anthony Fokker himself was soon in attendance with his ciné-camera and was able to record on film some of the activities over the next few days, including details of the second triplane victory, Sopwith Pup B1795 and its occupant, Lieutenant A. F. Bird, whom Richthofen brought down as his 61st victory on 3 September. Richthofen's first victory on the triplane had taken place two days earlier, when he approached an unsuspecting R.E.8 and shot it down from a range of 50 metres with only 20 shots. Doubtless the R.E.8 crew mistook Richthofen's machine for a Sopwith Triplane, an error of identification that would cause losses to both sides during the front-line indoctrination period of the Fokker triplane.

According to Fokker in *Flying Dutchman*, he spent some three weeks at the front, and although he states that this was shortly before Richthofen was killed, from the events he recounts there is no doubt that the period in question was August/September 1917. It may not have been a coincidence that the Voss activity recorded in the published war diary of Jagdgeschwader I** ceases for some ten days after he obtained his 47th victory on 11 September. This was Voss's ninth victory gained during

the period that 103/17 was with Jagdstaffel 10, but incomplete records do not show how many of these were on the triplane. It could indicate that Voss returned to Schwerin with Fokker to fly the production V 5 triplane. Since the exact date is not known, this move may even have been brought about by the loss of Wolff (promoted to Oberleutnant three days previously), who was shot down and killed in 102/17 on 13 September north of Wervicq in a combat against a number of British aircraft. Voss would have been keen to compare the Fokker Dr I, the type JG I was to receive as new equipment, with the V 4 triplane on which he had just obtained two weeks' operational experience. This would have been in keeping with Fokker's willingness to lend an attentive ear to what front-line pilots had to say about his products, and to consider any ideas for improvement. Since Richthofen was in Germany at that time, it is possible that he also came to Schwerin and partici-pated. Obviously, the reasons for the loss of 102/17 flown by such a capable pilot would have entered into the discussion. It is not known when Voss returned to the front, but in the evening of 23 September, after obtaining his 48th victory earlier in the day, he was shot down and killed in 103/17, crashing near Frezenberg on the British side of the lines during a fight against seven S.E.5a's of No 56 Squadron. This was strangely similar to the loss of Wolff, in that both triplanes were fighting against overwhelming odds.

Voss's last fight has been dramatically described by James McCudden, one of Britain's most knowledgeable and successful First World War fighter pilots; it was the earliest account of the fantastic manoeuvrability of the triplane.† McCudden wrote: 'The German pilot turned in a most disconcertingly quick manner . . . a sort of half flat spin . . . although I got behind him a second time, I could hardly stay there for a second. His movements were so quick and uncertain that none of us could hold him in sight [in our sights] at all for any decisive time.' Voss was obviously exploiting the lightning right-hand turn and also possibly resorting to flick manoeuvres. McCudden does not mention the climbing ability of the triplane, but other participants in the fight reported that Voss continually zoomed above the circling British fighters during the combat, and that he could have climbed out of reach of the S.E.5a's and got away. But Voss was made of sterner stuff and remained engaged, eventually damaging all the British aircraft, some of them severely. Whether he overstressed his controls in the peculiar flat skidding turns that he employed, exhausted his fuel, or for any other reason, in the end,

*Aircraft of experimental or new type were not included in the strength of a Jagdstaffel – they were merely attached and the unit retained a full establishment of its previous aircraft type.
**Jagd in Flanderns Himmel* by Karl Bodenschatz, Verlag Knorth & Hirth GmbH, Munich, 1935.

†*Flying Fury* by James McCudden, VC, DSO, MC, MM, John Hamilton, London, 1930.

▲ 46

▲ 47   ▼ 48

46. Triplanes of Jasta Boelcke lined up on Marcke aerodrome near Courtrai, late February/early March 1918. The Albatros D V on the right indicates that a full complement of triplanes had yet to be attained. The four nearest triplanes are (right to left): Vallendor's 195/17, Plange's 203/17, Loeffler's 190/17 and Baeumer's 204/17; these machines are detailed in individual photograph captions. All rear fuselages, tailplanes and elevators (top and bottom surfaces) display the unit marking in the Prussian colours of black and white, the colour division being on the aircraft centre-line.

47. Kempf's 213/17 in full warpaint leaves no doubt as to the identity of the aeroplane's pilot. His 'kennscht mi noch?' (Remember me still?) is in the 'alemannisch' dialect of his native Freiburg. Note that the undercarriage axle wing fairing has been modified by adding auxiliary struts.

48. Vizefeldwebel Paul Baeumer flew 204/17 (Works No 1923), which is seen at Marcke with a partly bordered rudder cross. The thin black rudder outline was a further display of the black and white Prussian colours, but not all Jasta Boelcke triplanes used it. The national insignia displayed on the top surfaces of the lower wing and on the tailplane are unusual, although a number of triplanes were so marked, and from the regular appearance of the wing crosses on this machine could have been factory-applied. The wing crosses on the bottom wing would soon be deleted, but the tailplane display was retained and eventually was changed to Balkenkreuz (straight-sided cross) style.

unable to evade the fire of 2nd Lieutenant Rhys Davids, he was shot down and killed.

When Voss was shot down he had been airborne for about 1½ hours. He had taken off at 18.05 German time, which was one hour ahead of British time (i.e., 17.05 British time), and was said to have crashed at 18.35 British time. Although the exact fuel tank capacity of the V 4 triplane is not known, other than an RFC Intelligence estimate of 'approx. 18 gallons' (82 litres) made from an examination of the remains of 103/17, it is known that the V 5 triplane carried 16 gallons (72 litres). The British found that 103/17 was powered by 110hp Le Rhône No T6247J, the engine that had been fitted to Nieuport 17 A6693 flown by Lieutenant E. J. D. Townsend of No 60 Squadron, RFC, who was reported missing on 5 April 1917. If Voss's tank was of 72 litres capacity (and the tank was full at departure), since the average fuel consumption of the 110hp Le Rhône was 10½ gallons per hour (48 litres), after 1½ hours' flight, some of it at full throttle during his initial climb and

when dog-fighting, fuel exhaustion may well have been the cause of his downfall.††

Fuel consumption varied with altitude and whether or not the engine was run at full throttle, but normal handling was to run the engine at 1,200rpm and this would consume fuel at the rate mentioned. If, indeed, the V 4 had the tank capacity given by RFC Intelligence (82 litres), there is no way of being certain that the tank was completely full when Voss took off. Furthermore, violent dog-fighting manoeuvres with a low fuel level in the tank, which supplied a simple gravity feed fuel system, could have starved the engine, causing it to stop at a critical time.

††The average fuel consumption of the Oberursel UR II was slightly better than that of the Le Rhône and was 46 litres per hour at full throttle. The amount of fuel carried in the Fokker Dr I (72 litres) was expected to provide for 1½ hours full throttle running at sea-level. During the ZAK acceptance tests mentioned earlier, it was permissible (and the weight schedule was so annotated) to reduce the amount of fuel on board to that required for one hour only. This was to provide a realistic mean weight for measuring the climbing performance. Operationally, of course, full tanks would normally be used.

STRUCTURAL FAILURE

THE first Fokker Dr I to be dispatched to the front was 115/17 (Works No 1783) on 4 October, and it was destined for Leutnant Heinrich Gontermann, Staffelfuehrer of Jasta 15 based at La Neuville in the VII Armee area. This aircraft was obviously intended to introduce the type into that Army and according to the War Diary of Jasta 15 115/17 arrived on 11 October 'from the Fokker Works in Schwerin'; thus again this may have been a direct shipment and not necessarily via AFP VII. The Dr I was assembled and ready to fly on 12 October, but Gontermann was ill for some ten days and did not fly the triplane until 26 October, which he did despite prevailing bad weather. His letters show that he considered the triplane 'fabulous' and he hoped that it would prove itself better on the front than those flown by Wolff and Voss. 'In any case, with mine I will take my time and feel my way with caution.'

In the IV Armee area it was apparently intended to ensure that a complete Jagdstaffel was equipped with the triplane on re-introducing the type, since of the twelve triplanes accepted during September, all but Gontermann's 115/17 were held at Schwerin before being dispatched, together with another six machines accepted early in October, to Jagdstaffel 11 in two

shipments on 10 and 13 October respectively. This seventeen-aircraft strong delivery (104/17, 106/17, 107/17, 109/17–114/17, 116/17, 118/17, 119/17, 121/17–123/17, 125/17 and 132/17) would probably have arrived at Marckebeeke around 20 October. Because the destination was not in doubt, there would be no need to transit this consignment of triplanes via AFP IV at Ghent. So, like the initial two Fokker triplanes, it was probably sent directly to Richthofen at Courtrai, where railway sidings were adjacent to Marckebeeke aerodrome.

The Jagdgeschwader Stab (Staff) was not usually a flying element, unlike a Stabskette (Staff Flight) which provided aircraft for the Kommandeur (Commander), Offizier zur besondere Verwendung (Adjutant – OzbV) and the Technisches Offizier (Technical Officer – TO). In such units, the OzbV and the TO were either not pilots or were 'ausgekaempft' (unfit for operational flying due to health reasons). In JG I the OzbV, Oberleutnant Bodenschatz, was not a pilot and Leutnant Krefft, the TO, does not feature on flying operations; he probably fitted into the latter category and was no longer an operational pilot. If, as seems possible, Jagdstaffel 11 at that time was expected to have the Kogenluft establishment of 21 aircraft (see later), the next bulk dispatch from Schwerin of five triplanes

▲ 49

49. Baeumer in front of 204/17 (the cowling front of which is still unpainted) with his mechanics (left to right):

▼ 50

Unteroffizier Henke, Baeumer, Gefreiter Meissner and Monteur Stahlmann. The aircraft was probably powered by a Beute (captured) Le Rhône engine, hence the use of a Nieuport-type propeller. A number of triplanes used such propellers and they may have been produced in Germany, but the lack of any German propeller manufacturer's trademark transfer on the propeller blades suggests the former origin. Undercarriage axle wing auxiliary bracing has been fitted to this triplane.

50. Leutnant Otto Loeffler with 190/17 (Works No 1908), one of a number of triplanes that he flew during his thirteen months' service in Jasta Boelcke. He was officially credited with 15 victories and was shot down twice, on the latter occasion in No Man's Land only a few metres from the British trenches. The colour of his fuselage band, flanked by two thin white stripes, was reportedly lemon-yellow, the colour of his old regiment, Grenadier-Regiment Koenig Friedrich Wilhelm II Nr 10.

(117/17, 124/17, 126/17, 127/17 and 138/17) on 29 October would have achieved this and also provided an aircraft for the JG Kommandeur. But before they could arrive, serious accidents resulted in the Fokker Dr I being taken out of service.

The introduction of the triplane in Jasta 11 was associated with difficulties, and during the last five days of October a pilot was lost on conversion flying in a Fokker D V; Vizefeldwebel (Acting Sergeant Major) Lautenschlaeger in 113/17 (Works No 1781) was shot down by mistake and Richthofen wrote off 114/17 (Works No 1782) when he was forced to land (apparently due to engine trouble, possibly the loss of a cylinder, since a photograph of his crashed machine shows that it had lost its engine cowling in flight). Finally, on 31 October, Leutnant Pastor was killed when the top wing of 121/17 (Works No 1832) failed in the air. Details of the events that led to this final accident appeared to be similar to those that had occurred the previous day with 115/17, when Leutnant Gontermann died from injuries received when he crashed on La Neuville aerodrome. They obviously warranted investigation. The triplane was grounded and came under the scrutiny of a ZAK Sturzkommission (crash commission) whose findings are given in Appendix I.

It is relevant to examine more closely the factors that caused the wing failures and the corrective action that was taken to prevent any recurrence. (Reference should also be made to the relevant wing layout drawings contained in the Appendix.)

Information from Fokker records indicates that the wooden interplane struts on the V 5 triplane were 'nur gegen Fluegelverdrehung' (only against wing twisting). The use of the word 'only' means that the struts did not contribute to the strength of the wing cellule, and that the individual wings were completely cantilever structures. Knowing the reason for the existence of the struts, when we examine aspects of wing twisting we see that the single interplane strut used to combat this was not completely effective, but was the only method that could be used with the double box spars closely connected together into what was, in effect, a single-spar layout. It is considered that the movement of the centre of pressure and the reaction of the wing structure to aileron operation were factors in Fokker Dr I top wing failures and that their effects contributed to the overstressing of structures that no longer possessed their full design strengths.

CENTRE OF PRESSURE MOVEMENT: To understand the forces acting on a wing, it is necessary to appreciate that the amount of lift generated depends on the angle that the wing makes with the airflow – called the angle of attack – and that a resultant of this lifting force is considered to act through a point which is called the centre of pressure. In a wing with a single spar, this component carries the whole load, and when the lift is greatest (at an angle of attack of approximately 15°) the centre of pressure is directly in line with the spar and only flexural bending is experienced. But at very low angles of attack – e.g., in a dive – the centre of pressure moves aft and inflicts a twisting force on the wing. This torsion is applied to the wing spar via the fabric covering and the rib portions behind the spar and acts directly on the rib attachments to the spar. Because of this, in a single-spar wing, especially one of light structure, considerable twisting of the wing aft of the spar can occur. The amount of movement of the centre of pressure depends on the shape of the aerofoil section, and in the deep thick aerofoil with slight undercamber used on the Fokker triplane (which was later given the designation Goettingen 298) this movement was sufficient to cause the variations mentioned.

AILERON REACTION: The point in the section of the wing where an applied force causes flexure without twist is called the flexural axis. A moment is produced about this axis when the ailerons are moved and this twists the wing in such a way that it reduces the aerodynamic forces brought into action. For example, if the aileron moves up, the aerodynamic force at the rear of the wing is downwards, giving a nose-up moment about the flexural axis; thus the angle of attack is increased, so producing an increased upwards reaction, while the down-going aileron on the other side of the wing produces a similar but opposite force at the same time. In a wing which is not sufficiently stiff in torsion, this phenomenon can actually produce a reversal of control. Despite the rigidity of the double box spars, covering the wing with fabric allowed a certain amount of twisting when the ailerons were deflected.

The short-span V 4 triplane apparently gave no great incidence of wing twisting when the ailerons were operated, but with the increased span of the modified V 4 and the V 5 with the use of greater area aerodynamically balanced ailerons, this was more pronounced. To prevent the twisting of the wing structure and to preserve the aileron effectiveness, interplane struts were fitted between the box spars. Now, when the ailerons were deflected, the spars twisted less than previously, but the force was still there, only it was now acting more directly on the auxiliary spars to which the ailerons were hinged, and to the ribs and rib attachments to the box spar. In the normal two-spar wing with internal drag bracing, especially in the braced cellule of a biplane, this would have been of little importance, but

51. Leutnant Wilhelm Papenmeyer and his second mechanic, Monteur Ziegler, with 214/17 (Works No 1933), which is marked with fuselage bands in the German colours of black-white-red. Papenmeyer used this machine for some six weeks from 28 January 1918 and obtained his third confirmed victory in it on 24 February. Note the light-coloured oblong on the over-painted black tailplane half, which suggests that 214/17 may have initially also been marked with a tailplane cross in the same manner as Baeumer's 204/17.

▼ 52

52. Leutnant Richard Plange with 203/17 (Works No 1922), marked with an additional iron cross insignia on the fuselage sides and decking on a light-coloured band immediately ahead of the usual fuselage national insignia. The distinctive shape of the Axial propeller usually fitted to the triplane's Oberursel UR II engine is apparent, its blades decorated by the manufacturer's trademark transfers.

53▲

54▲

53. Papenmeyer's 214/17 was so extensively damaged by bomb splinters during a British bombing raid on Marcke aerodrome on 13 March that the machine was written off. Jasta Boelcke experienced other losses during this attack, including five mechanics killed.

54. Papenmeyer's second triplane, 409/17 (Works No 1993), which he first flew operationally on 14 March. Fourteen days later he was

Baeumer's mechanic, Monteur Stahlmann, was one of the wounded.

54. Papenmeyer's second triplane, 409/17 (Works No 1993), which he first flew operationally on 14 March. Fourteen days later he was

forced to land in No Man's Land after shooting down an R.E.8 north of the Douai-Arras road. He was observed to vacate the aircraft but was found dead four days later by German infantry. Note that this aircraft carries the black-white-red fuselage bands

55▼

further aft than on his first machine.

55. Pilots of Jasta 36 at Kuerne aerodrome, early 1918. Left to right: Vizefeldwebel Patzer (left of cowling), Leutnant von Haebler (right of cowling), Vizefeldwebel Meyer, Leutnant Wandelt, Staffelfuehrer Leutnant Heinrich Bongartz, Leutnant Naujok, Leutnant Fuhrmann and Unteroffizier Huebner. The above identification is that given by Bongartz in the 1930s. However, there is an anomaly in that the aircraft is Fokker Dr I 465/17 (Works No 2091), which was accepted by BA 13 at Schwerin on 22 January 1918, and if dispatched without delay, could hardly have been with Jasta 36 before the beginning of February – yet Leutnant Gustav Wandelt of the unit was killed east of Staden on 23 January 1918. Thus there may have been an error in the Idflieg acceptance date or the officer above, on Bongartz' right, has been incorrectly identified. Note auxiliary strut bracing on undercarriage axle wing fairing.

56. Leutnant Johann Janzen, Jasta 6, early 1918 with 403/17 (Works No 1987). This pilot flew a number of triplanes during his nine months with JG I, becoming the Staffelfuehrer of Jasta 6 on 28 April. He had an amazing escape on 9 May during a fight with an S.E.5a. A single bullet severed all the control cables of his triplane's rudder and ailerons, causing him to fall completely out of control. A strong westerly wind drifted his spinning machine some 5km behind the German lines where it eventually crashed into a marshy area near the River Somme. Janzen, who was unhurt but admits to suffering some shock from this unnerving experience, was flying without the benefit of the recently introduced Heinecke parachute. Two days later he was airborne in a new triplane and continued to add to his victory score, which stood at 13 confirmed victories by 9 June, the day that he came down behind the French lines in one of the new Fokker D VII biplanes and became a PoW.

▲ 56

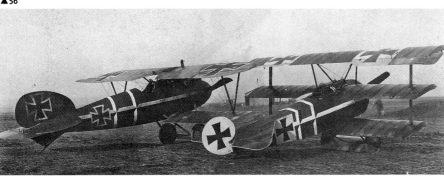

▲ 57   ▼ 58

57. When Jasta 14 based on Boncourt aerodrome in the VII Armee area received Fokker Dr Is in January 1918, markings previously carried on the unit's Albatros D Va's were transferred to the triplanes. As this was completed on 198/17 (Works No 1916), the machine selected by the Staffelfuehrer, Leutnant Hans Werner, he arranged for this photograph to be taken. The unit marking consisted of a horizontal black and white line from nose to tail, Werner's own marking being the two interlocking fuselage bands in the same colours. Note the very low ground clearance of the undercarriage axle fairing wing's trailing-edge.

58. Although 139/17 (Works No 1850) has equal-area ailerons, it was one of twelve triplanes dispatched from Schwerin on 12 December 1917 for Jasta 11, many of which were fitted with asymmetrical ailerons. It was one of five triplanes flown by Leutnant von Conta during February 1918 and is shown during this period on a visit to Jagdstaffelschule I (fighter school) at Valenciennes. This machine survived service with JG I until early May when it was transferred to Jasta 5, also based at Cappy, which was a ready recipient of surplus JG I triplanes.

this was not so on the triplane wing which had no internal bracing aft of the spar.

It has been seen that the strength of the Fokker triplane wing was adequate, and when the prototype Fokker F I 101/17 underwent its Bruchprobe at Adlershof, it passed this without difficulty. Obviously Fokker, knowing that this airframe would be tested to destruction in the structural strength tests, ensured that the standard of construction was high. It is also assumed that the airframe had not been subject to conditions conducive to the absorption of moisture by, for example, having been left out in the rain. In fact, the internal structure of the wings of 101/17 was not varnished, there being no need for such protection since its life was to be very short. This fact may even have prompted Fokker to adopt a less careful approach to this aspect during the manufacture of subsequent wings than he might otherwise have done, and this was the main cause of the initial wing trouble that manifested itself in October 1917.

One wonders if the same care given to the construction of the prototype wings attended series wing construction. If negligent building practices and lax inspection existed during the manufacture of production wings, there were specific areas in which the strength factor of the wing design could be eroded. These were:

1. Gluing and nailing procedures. ·
2. Composition of the cold-water glue. If in the interests of economy, this was mixed to an over-thin consistency, the strength of the joints would suffer.
3. Application of varnish to the completed wing structure before fabric covering. If a limited amount of varnish was allocated to each wing, uneven application would mean that some parts remained inadequately protected against the absorption of moisture.

Fokker triplane wings were made entirely of wood and their structural integrity relied, among other things, on the factors mentioned. Ribs attached to the spar, by gluing and nailing triangular-section wooden strips to them, provided the aerofoil shape. The aerodynamically balanced ailerons (of light-gauge steel tube welded construction) were hinged with three simple strap hinges to an auxiliary spar; this was attached to seven of the ribs by inserting the tails of the ribs into slots in the auxiliary spar, which was scalloped for lightness between these slots. The ribs at the ends of the auxiliary spar were mortise-joined to the spar, and the main attachment was via a double box rib adjacent to the cables for the aileron-operating horns.

Wings were covered in doped fabric, attached, as was normal German aeronautical practice, by nailing the fabric to the rib booms through a thin tape. Full depth stringing, whereby thin cord is run completely through the wing to secure the top and bottom fabric covers together along the whole rib outline, was not used. The complete fabric wing covering did not possess any drain holes for the removal of condensation. The only openings that could be considered for this purpose on the triplane were the holes for the aileron cables on the undersurface of the centre-section and those adjacent to the aileron-operating horns on both top and bottom wing surfaces.

While the quality of the wing covering fabric used by Fokker was reportedly sound, it is known that the same cannot be said for the dope used. Photographic evidence of quite short life Fokker airframes show cracks and whorls on doped surfaces. On the upper wing surface of the triplane, wing twisting could promote such fissures and lead to the ingress of moisture, which could not easily escape or evaporate. Inadequate internal varnishing allowed the entrapped moisture to soften glued joints and weaken the structure. This could precipitate failure, especially if the aircraft was subjected to the violent manoeuvres for which it was renowned. It should be remembered that pilots flew to the utmost of their ability and that they were not restricted by placarded limitations. Their actions were dictated by the gravity of the situation that they found themselves in, whether this was inspired by keenness to engage the enemy or the desire to evade him. There is no doubt that, on occasion, fierce handling overstressed airframes whose structures had already been weakened by any one or a combination of the factors mentioned.

Trouble usually started in the centre of the wing, probably due to the increased airflow velocity caused by the propeller slipstream.* Rib booms then worked loose from the rib webs. Since the fabric was attached to the rib booms, the lifting action of the airflow assisted this and tended to pull the upper rib booms off the rib webs if the glued joints were not adequate or their tenacity had been reduced by moisture. This caused ribs to buckle and become detached from the box spar, loosening the fabric, which was torn by the airflow, and disintegration of the wing commenced. In such a situation, if the ailerons remained intact, it was possible to nurse the aircraft to a landing. In fact, the control cable system was such that even if an aileron was lost, control of the

*The tips of the standard 2.62m-diameter Axial propeller were just above the lower nose contour of the top wing and despite the slight contraction of the slipstream diameter, which occurs a short distance behind the propeller, the lower wing surface doubtless came under its influence. The velocity of the slipstream at normal airspeeds is approx. 50 per cent higher than the speed of the airflow affecting those parts of the aeroplane outside the slipstream area and would impose a higher stress locally in the centre of the top wing.

▲59

59. Richthofen's 127/17 (Works No 1838) was dispatched from Schwerin on 29 October and as a result had to have its original wings replaced at the front. This work was probably undertaken at AFP IV. The period that the aircraft was out of service is not known, but may account for the fact that when this photograph was taken in late February on Phalempin aerodrome, when Richthofen visited Jasta 30, the machine was still basically in

▼60

factory finish. The engine cowling was undoubtedly painted red and a start has been made to update the national insignia by incorrectly painting out the white background of the rudder cross in camouflage colours to leave a 5cm-wide white border. This treatment should have been applied to upper wing and fuselage crosses, but not to the rudder, which should have been left as delivered.

60. Hauptmann Adolf Ritter von Tutschek, Kommandeur of JG II, carried out his first front-line flight on the triplane when he flew 216/17 (Works No 1935) on 19 February 1918. The aircraft is seen at Toulis in its original factory finish. The degree of streakiness of the Fokker greenish-brown camouflage varied with different aircraft, but was applied almost chordwise across the wings, vertically on the fuselage sides and

diagonally on the tailplane, elevators and fuselage decking. Components were painted individually and light and dark areas did not necessarly line up when the aircraft was assembled. The light-blue undersurface colour was extended around the lower longerons and on the tail unit, providing a uniform demarcation line between the colours.

remaining aileron was assured. Each aileron control cable system was a continuous loop; aileron operation did not rely on an interconnecting balance cable. Thus each aileron system was independent of the other, which meant that, with one aileron out of action, the aircraft could still be controlled laterally with the remaining aileron. While this could obtain in the event of combat disablement, it could not cope with the massive destruction of the upper wing experienced by both Gontermann and Pastor.

In the modifications demanded by Idflieg, the rigidity of the ribs and their attachment to the box spar were improved and the attachment of the auxiliary spar to the ribs also received attention; the 1.5mm-thick plywood ribs were each joined to the auxiliary spar by two triangular 'biscuits' of the same material. In addition, the scalloping of the auxiliary spar between the ribs was discontinued, and further to improve the attachment of the auxiliary spar, two double box ribs were fitted, one at each end of the auxiliary spar. The outboard double box rib also, of course, strengthened the wingtip itself, and this modification was extended to both the middle and bottom wings; these structures were also subject to deterioration due to the ingress of moisture, although generally to a lesser degree than the upper wing. The fabric covering was henceforth stitched to strips of fabric that had previously been attached to the rib booms, and the security of the rib booms to the rib webs was improved by transverse nailing, instead of merely relying on the adhesive properties of glue. It was realized that effective protection of the glued joints could only be maintained by the thorough application of varnish, and the need for greater care in this area was emphasized.

The ailerons were also modified, and the area of aerodynamic balance was reduced. The inverse taper, previously over the distance of two rib bays at the inboard end, now appeared over the last rib bay only, and this resulted in an increase of aileron surface area. Original ailerons were not discarded, but were used again after the size of their aerodynamic balances had been reduced; they were of course of smaller area than the new ailerons. Triplanes were fitted with both types when production was resumed, presumably until the stock of early ailerons was used up, and eventually the increased-area aileron became the standard on production machines. There was, however, an interim period when ailerons of both types were used on the same aircraft. When the aileron with the greater area was fitted on the port side, it is thought that this may have been an attempt to increase the rate of roll to the right and so further improve the triplane's lightning right-hand turn.

Several cases of structural failure of the top wing occurred even after the incorporation of the above corrective measures, but no documented accounts of further aileron loss are known. In this respect, at least, it appears that the modifications were satisfactory. However, the detachment of ribs and fabric in the centre of the top wing was to remain a possibility during the whole of the Fokker triplane's career.

It should be appreciated that this was the first operational aircraft whose wing structure relied solely on the integrity of glued wooden joints – there were no internal metal components in the triplane's wings. Provided that the workmanship was good, there was no reason for the wings to give any trouble; but the finish had to cater for the strenuous front-line conditions that the machine would encounter, especially proofing the wooden glued construction against the effects of moisture. Internal varnishing was only a partial solution, since it combatted moisture inside the wing. The real answer lay in more effective doping and weatherproofing of the wing fabric to prevent the ingress of moisture in the first place. One could hardly be expected to mollycoddle a front-line aeroplane, and the conditions in service were at times atrocious; in the mud of Flanders, where tents blew down in strong winds and driving rain, it was almost impossible to keep the machines dry. This was, of course, the reason why Richthofen demanded wooden sheds for JG I in November 1917 (see later) and also the reason why hangar tents were erected on Harbonnières landing ground in April 1918, despite that forward aerodrome being only some 8km from the front.

Despite the improved rigidity of the ribs occasioned by the Idflieg demands in November 1917, following the catastrophic failures of the upper wing, yet another problem arose with the Fokker Dr I wing structure in service. The leading-edge did not consist of a solid spanwise member, but was formed by thin plywood wrapped around the noses of the ribs, as already described. This was strong enough as long as it remained intact, but if punctured by enemy fire, airflow entering the wing tended to inflate the portion ahead of the full-depth plywood webs of the box spar. Increased internal pressure could then blow the fabric off the ribs and result not only in complete destruction of the leading-edge and that part of the wing ahead of the spar, but introduce failures that could spread to other parts of the wing.

In addition, air loads on the leading-edge could cause vertical fractures across the thin plywood rib webs, usually in the region of the large circular lightening holes, and allow portions of the plywood leading-edge to

61. Leutnant Walter Goettsch, Staffelfuehrer of Jasta 19, seated in 202/17 (Works No 1921) marked with a yellow '2', one of a seven-triplane consignment to VII Armee dispatched from Schwerin on 24 January 1918 for Jagdstaffeln selected to form JG II. The first triplanes of Jasta 19 generally used coloured fuselage bands and numerals for individual pilot identification, but Goettsch, who had come from Jasta 8 on 14 February, where he had used white as his Kette (Flight) marking, caused most pilot identification markings in Jasta 19 to be in this colour. He also instituted the deletion of fuselage national insignia further to identify the aircraft of his command and to prevent conflict with pilot identification markings.

62. The painting of the yellow '2' on the fuselage side of 202/17, which was also marked on the top decking aft of the cockpit, has obscured the military aircraft designation and serial number, and this has been re-marked, also in yellow, on the rear fuselage under the tailplane. Although the position of the re-marked information varied, this was a normal procedure in front-line units since it was required for 'book-keeping', and the painting of a pilot's identification marking often obliterated the factory-applied data. All components of the airframe bore the stencilled works number, but their loss due to over-painting was less important because this number was stamped into the metal manufacturer's plate riveted to the engine cowling. Another common practice in the field was to fit the wheels 'outside-in', which, due to the cone shape of the wheel disc, had the effect of widening the wheel track, a useful means of improving the aircraft's ground stability on rough aerodrome surfaces. This has been done here and 'Innen' (inside) can be

▲61

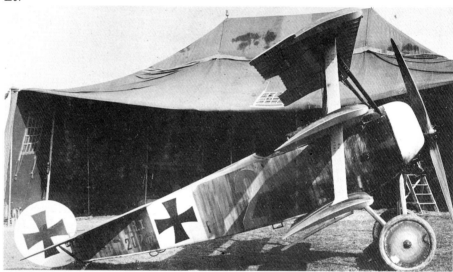

▲62

seen stencilled on the 'outer' fabric wheel cover.

▼63

63. Fokker triplanes suffered in various ways from the temperamental nature of their engines. The cowling of Goettsch's 202/17 has been all but torn off by the flailing action of a valve-operating pushrod which has worked loose. Another rotary engine ailment was 'blued' cylinders, caused by overheating due to faulty lubrication, which resulted in broken piston rings and partial seizure of pistons. In such cases the cylinder could be retrieved by lapping and a new piston fitted, but when several cylinders were 'blued' due to badly seized pistons an engine change was inevitable.

This was a relatively easy task, and after the disconnection of air, fuel and oil pipes, ignition wires and throttle linkage, only the four bolts of the steel tube pyramid engine mounting held the engine to the aircraft. Note the works number in front of the carburettor air intake. These stencilled numerals were only 3cm high and were difficult to read against the dark-painted forward fuselage, especially when that surface was contaminated with dirt and oil. The ease of legibility here indicates an almost new aeroplane.

64 ▲

64. Another early Jasta 19 triplane was 167/17 (Works No 1879) and this view of it on Cuirieux aerodrome in late February shows well the angle and proportions of the sloping black bands applied to the yellow tailplane and elevators (the centre of the tailplane left in its camouflage finish) that comprised the unit marking. The machine is marked with a

yellow '3', the thin white surround of the numeral being the chalk outline to guide the painter. This aircraft was also dispatched from Schwerin on 24 January and was one of the seven-triplane batch to AFP VII for units selected to form JG II. Note rear-view mirror.

65. Recently arrived 210/17 (Works No 1929) of Jasta 36 on Kuerne aerodrome near Courtrai. The machine has been raised into flying position with a trestle under the rear fuselage, and work is proceeding near the sternpost, possibly on the tailskid; this was a simple wooden member pivoted at this point at the bottom longerons, and sprung

by two rubber bungee cord loops at its upper end to the top longerons. The national insignia on the tailplane, auxiliary bracing struts on the aerofoil-section undercarriage wing and the circular access panel on the upper forward fuselage are features of Jasta 36 triplanes that are detailed in the text.

65 ▼

66. A pilot's own initial was not always used for identification of his aircraft, and such letters were often selected because of personal associations, usually with the opposite sex. The meaning of the styloform 'N' used by Leutnant Claus von Waldow of Jasta 15 as his personal marking is not known, but he had used it on previous aircraft types and in March 1918 at Autremencourt had it applied to his 412/17 (Works No 1996). Note the additional centrally mounted gunsights, raised above the normal aiming line.

▲66   ▼67

▼68

67. Recently arrived triplanes of Jasta 15 at Autremencourt, near Marle, in early March. Only the aircraft on the extreme right bears tailplane and elevator decoration, the chevrons of which proclaim it as the leader – probably the machine use by the Staffelfuehrer, Leutnant von Budde. Leutnant von Waldow's 412/17 marked 'N' is second from the left. The triplane on the extreme left with a black-bordered white band was probably flown by Leutnant Bergner, who used the same marking on his earlier Albatros DV. All aircraft have white engine cowlings, a marking carried at this time by all JG II triplanes, making it the first Jagdgeschwader marking. (A marking common to all triplane components of JG I and JG III was never used.) The rudders of the above aircraft would soon be over-painted, apparently in brown,

as a unit identification marking, leaving a narrow white border around the iron crosses.

68. Leutnant Monnington, the OzbV of Jasta 15, stood 401/17 (Works No 1985) on its nose in March 1918 during conversion to type. The triplane was accepted on 20 December 1917 and dispatched from Schwerin on 10 January as one of a batch of six to VII Armee for JG II. It is unusual that the interplane struts have been over-painted, obliterating the factory stencils and the location of the struts in the wing cellule re-marked in the non-standard fashion shown: O.L. = Oben Links (top left) and U.L. = Unten Links (bottom left). Equally unusual is the white arrow under the tailplane with the inscription 'Hier aufzubocken' (support here), showing the trestling position.

become detached, creating situations that could also lead to the disintegration of the wing structure. Curiously, Idflieg had asked that the large circular lightening holes in the plywood rib webs be discontinued, since they felt that their presence assisted the absorption of moisture; but Fokker did not incorporate this modification, no doubt feeling that adequate internal varnishing made it superfluous. A modification to the fore part of the wing ribs was introduced in March 1918, whereby the rearmost of the two large circular lightening holes in the ribs ahead of the spar was covered on each side by oblong plywood patches glued and nailed together. By this time Fokker triplane production had almost ceased, and since the incorporation of this modification to machines in the field would have been an involved process, it is thought that few if any triplane wings were so modified.

Three instances of upper-wing failure follow, while other examples are shown in photographs and detailed in their respective captions.

On 3 February Leutnant Joachim Wolff of Jasta 11 experienced failure of the leading-edge and ribs when flying 155/17 (Works No 1867) and was compelled to make a forced landing.

During the same month Unteroffizier Huebner of Jasta 36 found that the rear portion of his wing bent upwards throughout its entire span, and detached ribs caused a large area of fabric to tear loose in the airflow. The ailerons remained intact and he was able to land safely despite the impending total collapse of the wing.

On 10 May Leutnant Wenzl of Jasta 11, while taking violent evasive action to avoid colliding with another triplane in a dog-fight, overstressed his top wing, causing the failure of five ribs in the centre-section. Wenzl only noticed this some time afterwards when his triplane suddenly slowed down. As the damage developed due to the broken ribs, buffetted by the airflow, a large expanse of fabric was torn off and this exposed the internal wing structure, so creating a marked increase in drag.

JAGDGESCHWADER EQUIPMENT

THE Jagdstaffel was the tactical air-fighting unit and the general increase in aerial activity in 1917, with the attendant necessity of concentrating fighter forces, produced the first Jagdgeschwader. This was a permanent formation composed of four Jagdstaffeln under a permanent Kommandeur. It was directly at the disposal of the Armee-Ober-Kommando (Army HQ – AOK) and was to be used in especially threatened areas of the Army front to regain aerial superiority by attacking strong penetrations of enemy reconnaissance and bombing squadrons. Its use in this way ensured control of the upper air space, thus providing top cover for the lower-flying fighters of the other Army Jagdstaffeln operating in the specified Jagdraume (air-fighting areas) of the Gruppenkommandos (Corps HQs), which protected the two-seaters engaged on artillery observation and infantry co-operation.

Jagdgeschwader I was formed on 23 June 1917 when the overall command of Jagdstaffeln 4, 6, 10 and 11 was given to Richthofen. The effectiveness of a Jagdgeschwader depended in no small measure on the command qualities of its Kommandeur, and the good results obtained by JG I were without doubt due to Richthofen's leadership. A dearth of suitably qualified regular officers, with sufficient air-fighting experience to

command such units, was the main reason why the number of Jagdgeschwadern was not increased later in 1917. Instead, a system of non-permanent groupings of Jagdstaffeln was inaugurated in October 1917, each under the command of a Fuehrer der Jagdgruppe (Gruja) whereby the number of Jagdstaffeln in the Jagdgruppe varied according to the tactical situation, and this provided a similar means of operating concentrated fighter forces. However, the main difference between the Jagdgruppe and the Jagdgeschwader was that the Gruja generally managed and controlled the activities of his Jagdstaffeln by orders from the ground. These formations' results were much less effective than those achieved by a permanent fusion of four Jagdstaffeln under an airborne Kommandeur.

The value of the Jagdgeschwader at the disposal of the AOK was emphasized in a war-games study undertaken during the second half of 1917 by the Obersten Heeresleitung (German High Command – OHL) which, in conjunction with Kogenluft, saw the Jagdgeschwader as an essential component of the aviation forces to be placed at the disposal of an offensive Army having a front-line strength of twelve Divisions supported by another twelve Divisions in reserve. This strength equated to that already included in the preparations being made for the German Spring Offensive early in

69. Leutnant Hans Mueller of Jasta 15 with an unserviceable triplane, the number of which cannot be deciphered. The aircraft is marked with two thin white fuselage bands and its rudder is painted in the identifying unit colour, probably brown. The engine protection and partly removed propeller cover show that the machine has been out of use for a period, while the open bottom tray fuselage panel hints at trouble inside. Note that the typical Bremskloetze (chocks) have ropes attached for pulling them clear of the wheels; German chocks normally had just an iron handle and were removed by hand, despite the nearness of the rotating propeller.

70. On 13 March 1918 Leutnant Lothar von Richthofen, Staffelfuehrer of Jasta 11, suffered an upper wing leading-edge failure on 454/17 (Works No 2079), when diving steeply during a fight at 4,000 metres. Whether this was precipitated by violent handling or by enemy fire is not known. The resulting complete loss of the central wing structure is obvious and contemporary accounts (even Lothar's own) exaggerated the damage, giving the impression that the upper wing broke off and made a biplane out of the triplane! But the ailerons remained intact and Lothar

▲ 69

▼ 70

was able to glide under reasonable control until he tried to turn near the ground to avoid high-tension wires, when the machine stalled and crashed near Awoignt. The severity of the impact is apparent; it badly injured Lothar and kept him out of action for over four months. The oblong box in the centre of the top wing spar was a thin stripwood surround of the date of spar construction and the works serial number; these were painted on the spar and were visible through a celluloid panel sewn into the wing covering fabric, and this

panel can usually be seen in triplane photographs. These data were also roughly painted on the spar in larger numerals between number 5 and 6 ribs from the wing centre-line on the starboard side, and '13.12.17' and '2079' can just be read at this location on the original photograph. The unpainted ribbed panel attached to the forward top fuselage fairing for blast protection can be clearly seen under the left-hand gun muzzle, and this bears black powder stains at its forward edge. Lothar, who used the light yellow colour of his old

regiment, Dragoner-Regiment von Bredow Nr 4, as an identification marking, carried this on tailplane, elevators, rear fuselage and rudder, and also, as was normal for a leader in JG I, extended this colour along the top of the fuselage almost to the cockpit. The top surface of the upper wing was almost certainly also over-painted in light yellow, although it appears that at this time the square national insignia backgrounds were of a darker shade.

1918, which would utilize three such Armies (II Armee, XVII Armee and XVIII Armee). It was apparent that two additional Jagdgeschwadern would be required in order to allocate each of the attacking Armies such a formation.

The first organizational steps were now taken to create Jagdgeschwader II and Jagdgeschwader III so that they would be operationally ready for the opening of the Offensive on 21 March 1918, and Jagdstaffeln in both IV Armee and VII Armee were pre-selected for this purpose. Obviously the quality of the component Jagdstaffeln and the suitability of prospective Kommandeure were borne in mind. Before such formations could be assembled, it was necessary to ensure that sufficient aircraft of the type best suited to the main task of these AOK fighter forces were available. That the choice fell on the Fokker Dr I was understandable, since it was then considered to be the best German single-seater.

What made the Fokker Dr I particularly well suited to equip the high-flying Jagdgeschwadern was its climbing ability which, despite a falling-off in power of its rotary engine at altitude, meant that it could at least climb quickly to heights of around 5,500 metres – something that the other German fighters of the period, such as the Albatros D V and the Pfalz D III, could not.* Rate of climb was still seen as a more important attribute in a fighter aeroplane than mere speed, and although it was appreciated that the triplane was slow, height could be converted to speed by diving off a height advantage over an enemy; thus the speed deficiency was not considered to be too much of a handicap.

The initial order for 20 Fokker triplanes (100/17 – 119/17) placed on 14 July was a normal Idflieg procedure to evaluate production aircraft under operational conditions before placing larger orders. First deliveries of these aircraft had been expected at the end of August, but the shortage of engines caused delays and it was September before the first twelve Fokker Dr Is were accepted. It is believed that the decision to equip Jagdgeschwader I with the type was taken at this time and the second production order, this time for 100 machines (121/17 – 220/17), was placed in September to provide the numbers required.

It is necessary here to understand the difference between the Sollstaerke (planned establishment) of a Jagdstaffel, as used by Kogenluft, and the Iststaerke (actual tactical strength) that eventually obtained in these units. Kogenluft emphasis on the expansion of the fighter force, seen as essential for the spring of 1918, put the establishment of a Jagdstaffel at 21 aircraft, a figure that was never reached. Usually fourteen aircraft comprised the strength of such a unit formed before the 'Amerika-Programm' action, which resulted in doubling the number of existing Jagdstaffeln. These latter units, numbered from Jasta 40 upwards, actually only possessed strengths of some eight aeroplanes each. For planning purposes in late 1917, using the figure given, meant that the Sollstaerke of a Jagdgeschwader stood at $21 \times 4 = 84$ aeroplanes, and this may explain why 100 Fokker Dr Is were ordered at this time. That this unusually large number of aircraft was envisaged as the strength of a Jagdgeschwader was confirmed by Richthofen, who, refusing to use tents because of the wet weather, required wooden hangars for a new aerodrome location (presumably Avesnes-le-Sec/Lieu-St Amand, 14km north-east of Cambrai), had asked the Kogenluft technical officer, Oberleutnant von Falkenhayn, on 6 November 1917 for 80 Einsitzerhallen. These were standard sectional wooden flat-roofed sheds large enough for only one aeroplane and were transported to site and erected by special troops of the Hallenbau (hangar construction) organization. The reason that Richthofen did not ask for more than 80 sheds was because some suitable wooden hangars already existed on the west aerodrome at Avesnes-le-Sec.

Production of the triplane received a setback following the structural problems with the wings, and during November the factory had to replace all the wings that had previously been delivered. That Idflieg were completely satisfied with the rectification action and that their faith in the Fokker Dr I was unshaken is shown by a third, and final, order for the type being placed during this month; these additional 200 machines (400/17 – 599/17) were obviously to cater for the equipping of JG II and JG III. Meanwhile another triplane fighter with an even better climbing performance had emerged. This was the Pfalz Dr I powered by a 160hp Siemens und Halske geared rotary engine. Although reportedly not quite as manoeuvrable as the Fokker triplane, its advantage was that it could climb to 6,000 metres in $14\frac{1}{2}$ minutes. Type-tested at Adlershof in October 1917, it was planned to produce 100 machines of this type and introduce them to the front simultaneously in January 1918, doubtless as the equipment of a complete Jagdgeschwader. This procedure of hoarding a type until sufficient numbers were on hand, to make an impression by introducing a type of known superiority over the enemy, has already been mentioned. It was not possible to adopt this procedure with the Fokker Dr I because its

*The best climbing performance recorded by a production Fokker Dr I was obtained with 178/17 (Works No 1896), which reached a height of 5,000 metres in 15½ minutes on its acceptance test flight of 4 December 1917 (see Appendix III for further details).

71. When Fokker Dr I 163/17 (Works No 1875) was dispatched from Schwerin on 13 December 1917, it was apparently sent to Adlershof for some purpose, possibly associated with the wing modifications, and was photographed on the snow-covered aerodrome there in, possibly, early January 1918. It was eventually shipped to JG I at Avesnes-le-Sec where it came on the strength of Jasta 11 and was flown by several pilots. It is not known what pilot originated the black-bordered white band applied to the fuselage for individual identification, but during February the aircraft was flown in air-firing practice and operationally by Leutnant von Conta. During a front-line flight on 21 February von Conta made a successful forced landing in this machine, possibly due to engine trouble, which he rectified. He then took off to return to Avesnes-le-Sec, only to be forced down again, this time breaking the propeller and damaging the upper mainplane. The triplane is shown here when flown by Leutnant von Linsingen on 17 March while accompanying Richthofen on a visit to Jasta 5 at Boistrancourt; apart from a red engine cowling, it does not appear to have any further Jasta 11 decoration. The machine continued to be used by Jasta 11 until early May when it was disposed of to Jasta 34b at Foucaucourt, where the Staffelfuehrer, Oberleutnant Greim, first test-flew 163/17 on 11 May. He used it operationally on 18 May but was compelled to make a forced landing near Athies when a cylinder parted company with the rest of the engine.

72. When Richthofen visited Jasta 5 at Boistrancourt on 17 March, he used this Jasta 6 triplane 525/17 (Works No 2193). His meeting with the Jasta 5 Staffelfuehrer, Oberleutnant Flashaar, was doubtless to discuss operational details of fighter deployment in

▲ 71

▲ 72

▼ 73

the northern part of the II Armee area for the coming offensive, when Jasta 5 and Jasta 46 formed Jagdgruppe 2 and operated in conjunction with JG I. Note the unusual over-painted wingtip leading-edge markings, obviously in a highly contrasting colour, possibly yellow. The rectangular access panel on the forward fuselage ahead of the carburettor air intake is the standard pattern adopted by Jasta 6 and used on all its triplanes.

73. Richthofen with 525/17 at Boistrancourt on 17 March

talking to pilots of Jagdstaffel 5. Left to right: Rittmeister Manfred Freiherr von Richthofen, mechanic, Leutnant von Hippel, Oberleutnant Flashaar,

unknown, Leutnant Schloemer and Leutnant Lehmann. Note the disparity of the black and white stripes of the Jasta 6 unit markings on the tailplane.

production lacked the necessary concentration, due mainly to engine shortages and the structural problems that arose in service with the first machines. It also proved impossible to implement it with the Pfalz Dr I, since insurmountable engine problems led to only ten machines of the type being produced.

The reason why larger numbers of Fokker triplanes were not produced was the knowledge that better fighters would be available later in 1918, because of the effort being put into engine and aeroplane development brought about by the 'Amerika-Programm'. In this respect the triplane was probably considered to be a 'stop-gap' fighter. It certainly appears that the Fokker triplane was an expendable aircraft type, and from such records that remain there is no evidence that major repairs were carried out to crashed airframes, either by Fokker or by any of the recognized repair companies. Although the steel tube components, such as the fuselage, tailplane and control surfaces, were repairable, except in extreme cases, the wing structure was not. To retain the necessary strength of the cantilever box spars, any repairs to them would have to be carried out with extreme care; the flimsy plywood parts of the rest of the wings were probably better discarded. Thus, because of the style of construction, repairs were not practically feasible. No doubt minor repairs and the cannibalization of undamaged components at both unit and AFP levels were carried out, and this would have extended the useful life of some machines.

Fokker production, having got off to a bad start, never caught up with front-line demands, and insufficient numbers of triplanes were available early in 1918 completely to equip the twelve Jagdstaffeln of JG I–III even to the normal strength of fourteen aircraft each. At the beginning of the Spring Offensive on 21 March, none of these AOK fighter formations possessed a full triplane complement. Apart from the shortage of aircraft, by this time other operational factors decreed that some of the component Jagdstaffeln continue to operate their original equipment. In April, as more triplanes became available, this philosophy did not materially change and these now additional triplanes were used to ensure that the existing Jagdstaffeln with the type had a good supply of replacement aircraft. This was necessary because triplane attrition was abnormally high, due mostly to the unreliability of its engine. Thus there was no shortage of triplanes at this time. Had this situation occurred some two months earlier, the three Jagdgeschwadern would have been completely equipped with the type as had originally been planned.

As already stated, sufficient triplanes were ordered to equip the three Jagdgeschwadern to strengths equating to the Kogenluft planning figure. Apart from the shortage of aircraft making this an impossible goal, practical experience showed that the sizes of such assemblies of aircraft were unwieldy, and smaller numbers of aircraft were more easily handled in the air by the formation leaders. Richthofen himself considered that Ketten (Flights) of from six to seven aeroplanes were best, and two such sub-units put the component Jagdstaffeln strengths of the Jagdgeschwadern at from twelve to fourteen machines; thus the tactical strength of a Jagdgeschwader comprised some 50 aircraft.

Flights in such strengths were not an everyday occurrence. They were only necessary when strong enemy formations had to be countered and were a means of bringing large numbers of aircraft into contact with the enemy. If the Allied formations were split up by the intensity of the Jagdgeschwader attack, fighting then developed into a number of individual combats, and the re-assembly of the aircraft into an orderly JG formation after such fighting, in order to continue the flight in sufficient strength, was one of the most difficult operations to achieve. Individual aircraft, split up by combat and unable to find their own Jagdstaffel, were under orders to return to their bases, to lessen the risk of unnecessary losses. When enemy air activity was such that the use of the Jagdgeschwader in strength was not required, sorties were made with individual Jagdstaffeln, or even Ketten, and the major part of the JG work was done at such strengths. However, when strong enemy aerial activity demanded, the Jagdgeschwadern were able to put up the large formations which were then necessary due to the numerical and technical superiority of the enemy aeroplanes.

JAGDGESCHWADERN I–III

RE-EQUIPMENT of certain Jagdstaffeln with the Fokker Dr I early in 1918 indicates that they were intended to become components of JG II (VII Armee) and JG III (IV Armee). In some cases transition training of these units from their stationary-engined Albatros D V and Pfalz D III fighters began in

74. The bulky standard German 'Fliegerkombination' (flying suit), tucked into the thigh-length flying boots which were worn over normal footwear, is seen to advantage in this view of Leutnant Hans Mueller of Jasta 15 with 218/17 (Works No 1937) at Autremencourt. Note the information board hoisted by means of a wooden pyramid and indicating the serviceability state or availability of the four triplanes currently on charge. 'Start' is an abbreviation for 'startklar' (ready for flight), while the use of 'Res.', apart from meaning in reserve, probably also infers that these aircraft were 'unklar' (unserviceable) at the time. Note also how the manufacturer's data plate on the engine cowling has been left unpainted.

75. Hauptmann Wilhelm Reinhard, Staffelfuehrer of Jasta 6, standing by his damaged triplane in mid-March. The broken box spars, missing right-hand wingtip and aileron, and the crushed rudder are the results of the aircraft somersaulting onto its back during what must have been a hectic landing, caused by structural failure of the upper wing when most of the upper surface fabric had been lost. Reinhard is holding the harness of his Heinecke parachute in his right hand. The fact that he opted for landing instead of abandoning the aircraft indicates that it must have been under reasonable control, although at this time pilots viewed the recently issued parachutes with distrust, and were reluctant to use them even in situations like this.

76. Six white-tailed triplanes and an Albatros D V of Jasta 13 on Reneuil-Ferme aerodrome, March 1918, shortly before flying to Guise aerodrome in the XVIII Armee area, where the component Jagdstaffeln of JG II concentrated before the opening of the Spring Offensive

▲74

▲75 ▼76

on 21 March. Pilot identification markings in this unit were confined to fuselage symbols marked between the forward limit of the white area and the cockpit. The triplane with its tail raised into flying position and with wavy band marking was flown by Leutnant Pippart, later to become the Staffelfuehrer of Jasta 19.

56

January, when pilots were familiarized with the different engine handling and flying characteristics of rotary-engined aeroplanes by undertaking practice flights in Fokker D Vs that had been allocated to them.* Since this type was not cleared for operational use, these machines were additional to the established strengths of the Jagdstaffeln concerned. When triplanes did arrive, it appears that they were generally assigned in small numbers initially. Thus units continued to operate their original Albatros D Vs and Pfalz D IIIs until sufficient triplanes were on hand to replace them. Mixed equipment was common in many of the component Jagdstaffeln until April, and the idea of completely equipping all three Jagdgeschwadern with the triplane did not materialize for a number of reasons.

The Jagdgeschwadern were always to be found where the fighting was hottest. They had no place in the relatively placid surroundings of static warfare. Thus their transfer to a new part of the front always heralded a new offensive. In the following brief accounts of JG I–III, covering the offensive actions of March–June 1918, the aerodromes used by their component Jagdstaffeln, until their use of the triplane terminated, are given. Reference should also be made to the map in Appendix VIII, to appreciate where the German offensive actions took place during this period.

JAGDGESCHWADER I

Following the grounding of the triplane, Jasta 11 had to revert to its previous Albatros D Vs and it was not until late December 1917 that the first consignment of triplanes with the modified wings arrived (137/17, 139/17, 142/17–148/17, 150/17–154/17 and 156/17, dispatched from Schwerin on 12/13 December). When the previously assigned aircraft were fitted with new wings and reissued to JG I from AFP IV is not known, but it is thought that this did not happen until February. Jasta 11 was equipped with the triplane by early January and Jasta 6 soon followed. However, both units still had a number of Albatros D Vs on charge and used these

operationally, alongside the triplanes, until well into February. Jasta 4 and Jasta 10 continued to operate the Albatros D Va and Pfalz D IIIa, no attempt being made to replace these types with triplanes, and it is worth considering the reasons for this.

When fully equipping a formation the size of a Jagdgeschwader with a new aircraft type, especially one that had already shown technical shortcomings, there was always the risk that similar or other problems would present themselves, and this might lead to the grounding of the aircraft, effectively putting the whole Jagdgeschwader out of action. Richthofen had by now become disillusioned with rotary engines, mainly because of their unreliability caused by having to use poor quality lubricating oil. Consequently he was not interested in having higher-powered rotaries, even of 200hp, in JG I. He was also well aware of the development of new fighter types. In fact, during January he had flown the forerunner of what became the Fokker D VII (powered by a 160hp Mercedes D III six-cylinder water-cooled in-line engine) at the D-Flugzeug Wettbewerb (fighter biplane competition) at Adlershof. He realized that its performance was not much better than, and its manoeuvrability not as good as, the triplane he was using; but he was aware of plans to fit the new aircraft with improved engines, such as the 185hp BMW and the high-compression Mercedes of similar power output, and he wanted such machines for JG I.

Production of the Fokker D VII would have allowed Richthofen to have obtained sufficient aircraft of this type to have equipped two Jagdstaffeln early in April, but these would not have had the higher-powered engines, and he probably told Idflieg that he did not want them, preferring to wait a few days longer for the desired versions. Since the Fokker D VII was not forthcoming, Jasta 4 was belatedly equipped with triplanes on 20 April. Jasta 10 never received the Fokker Dr I. It appears that isolated examples were operated by Jasta 10, presumably for specific duties, such as attacks on observation balloons, when pilots and their triplanes from Jasta 6 or Jasta 11 were attached to Jasta 10 for varying periods. But it seems that the reason why Richthofen kept Jasta 10 flying stationary-engined fighters after mid-April was that he was hoping daily to receive Fokker D VIIs at least in sufficient numbers to equip a complete Jagdstaffel. Apart from the preference for the higher-powered Fokker D VII, which would not in any case be available for another two months, the official policy of harbouring a new aircraft type at storage depots before releasing them to the front in number may have been the real reason why Richthofen could not get Fokker D VIIs in April.

*During the period that Fokker triplanes replaced stationary-engined biplanes of the Albatros and Pfalz types in the Jagdstaffeln, the earlier Albatros D V and Pfalz D III were being superseded by the improved Albatros D Va and Pfalz D IIIa. Unless it is known that the later specific types were in use by the unit concerned, the terms Albatros D V and Pfalz D III are used in the text.

The degree of change in the numbers of each aircraft type at the front is shown in the following table extracted from the record of front-line strengths on the last day of the months quoted:

December 1917		*February 1918*	
Albatros D V	513	Albatros D V	250
Albatros D Va	186	Albatros D Va	475
Pfalz D III	276	Pfalz D III	182
Pfalz D IIIa	114	Pfalz D IIIa	261

▲77

77. Although this postcard photograph has suffered from retouching, it is an important document and shows nine triplanes of Jasta 11 on the landing ground at Awoingt, south-east of Cambrai, during the Spring Offensive and before moving to Léchelle. The triplanes were deployed to Awoingt from Avesnes-le-Sec during the afternoon of 20 March. Leutnant von Conta ferried 477/17 (one of Richthofen's reserve machines) and his own then current triplane, 107/17 (Works No 1775). Other pilots made similar flights until all the regular and reserve triplanes were in position for the following day's attack. On the extreme left the Albatros D Va's and Pfalz D IIIa's of Jasta 4 can be seen, their fuselages decorated with the unit's black spiral stripe marking.

▲78 ▼79

78. Leutnant Keseling of Jasta 10 was brought down by ground fire and captured on 24 March, flying 147/17 (Works No 1859) which was a Jasta 11 machine (note the circular door for access to the oil pump described elsewhere). The guns and top forward fuselage fairing have been removed, revealing the ammunition feed guides with loaded belts still in place. The four tubular forked brackets on which the guns were mounted can be seen; also the Maximall fuel contents gauge. The 10mm-thick black horizontal line on the fuselage under the officer's hand is the rigging datum and is painted on the fuselage on the engine thrust line.

79. Hauptmann von Tutschek flew 404/17 (Works No 1988) from late February. This is an early photograph before the tail unit black was extended to border the rudder and fuselage national insignia and shows a mechanic about to swing the propeller, while another stands by the tailplane, ready to hold it down when the engine starts. Tutschek's white cloth for wiping oil from his goggles can be seen tucked under the right-hand strap of his shoulder harness. The telescopic Oigee sight has yet to be fitted. Unteroffizier Balzer, Tutschek's leading mechanic, is standing by the cockpit.

80. On parade! The reason that all the aircraft of Jasta 12 were neatly lined up on Toulis aerodrome on 15 March 1918 was because of the visit of official Kogenluft photographers. In this early morning scene JG II's Kommandeur, Hauptmann von Tutschek (wearing a ¾-length British leather flying coat), is standing in front of the assembled mechanics beyond the starboard wingtips of his black-tailed triplane (404/17), the machine in which he was killed a few hours later. To the left of Tutschek's triplane can be seen the Albatros D V and the triplane that is replacing it flown by the Jasta 12 Staffelfuehrer, Oberleutnant Blumenbach: both machines were marked with a horizontal white stripe with an intersecting white band around the fuselage aft of the cockpit.

81. The other end of the Toulis line-up. The aircraft types are arranged alternately since one of each type shared the same hangar tent, and were the machines of one pilot. Personal markings carried on the Albatros are in the process of being marked on the triplanes. Several 'pairs' can be identified; the two aircraft nearest the camera, marked with a black-bordered white chevron, were the machines flown by Vizefeldwebel Ulrich Neckel.

82. Aerial view of the Toulis line-up showing ten triplanes. Some have only recently arrived since they have still to be marked with the black rear fuselage and tail unit which, combined with the white engine cowling already applied, comprised the Jasta 12 unit marking.

83. Three black-tailed triplanes at Toulis, March 1918. Behind Tutschek's 404/17 with its leader's streamers can be seen Oberleutnant Blumenbach's 217/17 (Works No 1936), marked with his horizontal white stripe. The aircraft nearest the camera is 436/17 (Works No 2061), flown at this time by Leutnant Hoffmann. Both 217/17 and 436/17, which were accepted at Schwerin on 25 and 12 January respectively, would survive several months of hard usage and were both still on the strength of Jasta 12 in June, when Leutnant Greven flew 436/17 on several occasions.

▲ 83

▲ 84   ▼ 85   ▼ 86

84. Preparing Hauptmann von Tutschek's 404/17 for flight. The mechanic standing on the right-hand wheel, apparently checking the oil tank filler cap for security, is Unteroffizier Balzer. Being in charge of the Kommandeur's aeroplane, he is also no doubt keeping an eye on the mechanic in the cockpit who, having lifted the Kastendeckel (breech cover) of the right-hand gun to gain access to its bolt mechanism, is obviously from the Waffenmeisterei. The internal moving parts of the LMG 08/15 required frequent lubrication, but the grease and oil for ground weapons had little application in aerial use and a special oil with a low freezing point (MG Oel 16) was used.

85. Apparently Leutnant Paul Hoffmann of Jasta 12 flying 436/17 at Toulis in March 1918. He was severely wounded in the stomach and pelvis on 1 April during a fierce combat near Montdidier, presumably in this machine. He managed to return and land safely at Balâtre but died of his wounds the following day.

86. Leutnant Oskar Mueller, the Technical Officer of JG II, was no longer an operational pilot in March 1918 when this photograph was taken. He had flown two-seaters since 1915, but was now considered to be suffering from Kriegs-muedigkeit (war-weariness), and according to Hermann Becker never flew the triplane. He is seen at Toulis beside Oberleutnant Blumenbach's 217/17.

A letter that Richthofen wrote to his friend Oberleutnant von Falkenhayn on 2 April 1918 gives a good picture of the changing air-fighting scene, and the shortcomings of the triplanes in their attempts to engage the enemy, now flying at ever-increasing altitudes. Richthofen obviously used these shortcomings to highlight his urgent need for Fokker D VIIs with the high-powered engines; in fact, his letter starts by asking von Falkenhayn when he can expect such machines. He goes on to emphasize the superiority of the enemy single-seaters and two-seaters, and tells of high-flying fighters diving on the German formations that are already at their ceiling, zooming to stay above them, seldom giving the Germans a chance to engage them, and of the impossibility of reaching the high-flying two-seaters that dropped their bombs and carried out their reconnaissances unmolested. As well as altitude capability, speed had now become an essential requirement, and Richthofen felt that the Germans could have shot down 'five to ten times as many enemy aircraft as we did if only we had been faster'. He included an explanation of why during the recent offensive the low cloud base, which kept the triplanes manoeuvring at heights between 50 and 700 metres for two hours, had been a distinct advantage, since at those low heights the triplane was able to utilize its superiority. But, he added, had their machines been fitted with the high-compression Siemens rotary engines, they would not have been able to fly at all in these conditions.*

Richthofen also mentioned that aircraft attrition had become exceptionally high, because every emergency or forced landing in the old shelled area of the Somme resulted in a complete write-off. He stated that emergency landings often resulted after air-fighting and this was naturally causing a large number of crashes. What he did not mention, but was then a factor in the number of forced landings after air-fighting, was that it was not unusual for pilots to fly until they ran out of fuel. Under normal circumstances, such unfortunates usually found a suitable place to force-land, but that was seldom possible in the large devasted area of the Somme. The two hours of low-level manoeuvring mentioned in Richthofen's letter shows that the fighter sorties were taken to the extreme limit of the triplane's fuel and oil supply, thus the forced-landings were not always due to enemy action.

Jagdgeschwader I, assigned to II Armee, moved from its winter quarters with its wooden hangars at Avesnes-

le-Sec and Lieu-St Amand on 20 March, occupying the landing ground at Awoingt, 5km south-east of Cambrai. Following the opening of the offensive and the beginning of the advance, Richthofen, who chose to be well forward, right behind the fighting troops, was constantly on the look-out for suitable aerodromes for JG I, and had already selected Léchelle (10km south-east of Bapaume) as a base. Almost as soon as German infantry took this British aerodrome, triplanes of Jasta 6 and 11 were landing on it on 26 March. Because of the speed of the advance, Léchelle was soon 25km behind the lines and from 6 April JG I was using an advanced landing ground at Harbonnières (20km south-west of Péronne) with success, since enemy aerial activity could be seen from the aerodrome. The triplanes were ferried daily from Léchelle to this field, which was only some 8km behind the front-line, spending the whole day there before returning to Léchelle in the late evening. Pilots were kept at immediate readiness, sometimes sitting in their cockpits strapped-in, and could engage the low-flying enemy infantry co-operation and artillery observation aircraft within a very short time of their first being seen. To protect the triplanes from heavy rain showers, eight hangar tents were erected on Harbonnières, despite its close proximity to the front, and this precaution shows that there was still some concern over the effectiveness of the weatherproofing of their wing surfaces.

After the advance had come to a halt, Richthofen personally selected a large grass area 1–2km south-east of Cappy (10km west of Péronne) as a more permanent aerodrome, and this was prepared with the help of men from a machine-gun company and British PoWs. By 12 April, when JG I took up residence there, 40 hangar tents for the aeroplanes and 100 captured British Bell tents for the personnel had been pitched. Work then began on more permanent buildings, with the assembly of captured British Nissen huts. This activity ceased the following day when orders were given for JG I to proceed north to Lomme, 8km west of Lille, for the Kemmel Offensive with VI Armee, and ground personnel departed for Lomme. It was decided to fly the aircraft to the new location, but departure was delayed by two days of rain. During the first break in the weather, on 15 April as JG I was about to take off from Cappy – pilots were actually standing by their triplanes, and just as Richthofen was pulling on his seal fur flying-boots – a messenger on horseback arrived with a signal countermanding the movement order.

Richthofen was lost on 21 April during an engagement in which he followed a fleeing Sopwith Camel at low altitude behind the British lines. Controversy as to who

*This was because of the 'over-compressed' nature of the Siemens und Halske Sh III, to improve its performance at high altitude, and whose handling characteristics demanded that in order not to damage the engine, it should be run at reduced throttle settings in the lower levels.

87. Leaving Boncourt for Masny in preparation for the March Offensive, Leutnant Werner's 198/17 is taken from the aerodrome to the railway loading point. Almost all Jasta moves were by rail, even those of comparatively short distance. This was to keep the flying components and the ground support personnel and all equipment together as a coherent unit, which could easily be redirected as required. In this case, only some 130km were involved, but an added factor was the secrecy necessary in concentrating forces in the three attack armies. Detours of greater length were undoubtedly taken before Jasta 14 was able to move forward, in the XVII Armee area, to Masny aerodrome which was 15km behind the front-line.

88. Fokker Dr I 441/17 (Works No 2066) flown by Leutnant Heinrich Bongartz, Staffelfuehrer of Jasta 36. On 30 March 1918 he was wounded by anti-aircraft fire; whether the shellburst also inflicted the damage that caused the whole leading-edge of his aircraft's upper mainplane to break up is not known. The machine probably stood on its nose during landing, no doubt further damaging the leading-edge, and possibly explains the removal of engine, cowling and propeller which would also be damaged in such a landing; if not, they might have already been salvaged for further use. Note the section of leading-edge plywood with its upper surface serrations, wedged into the centre-section struts. This view shows to advantage two local modifications that were common to Jasta 36 triplanes, originating with that unit's Werkmeister: auxiliary struts fitted to the undercarriage axle fairing wing, and the provision of two access holes in the forward fuselage sides above the thrust line, covered by circular panels. These features were incorporated into Jasta 36 triplanes on arrival in the unit

▲ 87

and not carried out merely as a result of necessity during service. The obvious advantages of these two field modifications caused them to be adopted in varying degree by other units (see chapter on Maintenance).

89. Rear view of 441/17 shows the large area of loose and torn fabric of the upper mainplane and its almost complete absence of dope; poor adherence has caused most of the dope to flake off the surface of the fabric flapping in the airflow. The national insignia marked on the tailplane arose because of 'recognition difficulties' from certain angles with the triplane and was introduced at one period in IV Armee, being common in Jasta 36. From dead astern, when the top wing crosses were almost illegible, that on the tailplane (which was installed at approximately twice the wing angle of incidence) would still have been recognizable, although the black cross is not evident in this view due to light reflection. Bongartz, who was credited with 33 victories, was wounded for the sixth and final time in the air on 29 April 1918. Flying his reserve triplane, 575/17 (Works No 2245), in a fight with several British aircraft, he was hit in the head by a bullet

▼ 88

▼ 89

which went through his left temple, eye and nose. On the verge of unconsciousness, he landed his machine in the shell-

torn vicinity of Kemmel Hill. His aircraft was riddled with bullet holes, there being 38 hits in the engine cowling alone.

brought Richthofen down continues to this day. When his red triplane, flying low over the Australian positions, turned into the easterly wind, that visibly slowed its progress; thousands of bullets were being fired at his aircraft, and when it gave a convulsive jerk and began to descend, many believed that their shots had been the decisive ones. The triplane hit the ground in a level attitude with considerable force, bounced (according to eye-witnesses) some 10 feet into the air again, before coming to rest. Doubtless the initial impact not only collapsed the undercarriage, but also the centre-section struts of the top wing. This damage would not be apparent to a distant aerial observer and German reports stating that the triplane made a 'glatte Landung' (smooth landing) caused them to believe that Richthofen was still alive when he landed. German triplane pilots, knowing how sensitive this machine was to fly and the absolute impossibility of its landing unaided, were genuinely stunned to learn that he was dead, and for a long time it was thought that Richthofen had been killed on the ground. The landing, however, although on an even keel, was not as smooth as the German witnesses thought and considerable additional damage was inflicted on the machine by several hours of shell-fire, before it was eventually retrieved and set upon by the souvenir hunters. Richthofen's body was still in the wreckage over two hours after he had crashed at 10.50am.

Hauptmann Wilhelm Reinhard became Richthofen's successor as Kommandeur of JG I, which remained at Cappy until 20 May when it moved to Guise in the XVIII Armee for a few days to prepare for the Marne Offensive with VII Armee. Fokker D VII biplanes had begun to arrive while JG I was still at Cappy to replace the triplanes of Jasta 6 and 11 and the re-equipment was completed at Guise. Thus Jasta 4 was now the only triplane component of JG I. This unit, under Leutnant Ernst Udet, continued to operate the triplane with success from Puisieux-Ferme (5km north-east of Laon) and Beugneux-Cramoiselle (20km north of Château-Thierry) during the Marne Offensive, which commenced on 27 May, until mid-June, when Jasta 4 also received sufficient Fokker D VIIs for the triplanes to be given up to AFP VII.

JAGDGESCHWADER II

In the VII Armee it appears that four of its best Jagdstaffeln had been selected to be component units of JG II – Jasta 13, 14, 15 and 19. Earlier Jasta 15 had apparently been selected as the unit to introduce the triplane into VII Armee, when Leutnant Gontermann received 115/17. However, the loss of this aircraft and the disruption to Fokker Dr I production that followed seem to have prevented further allocations of the triplane to VII Armee, until January when Jasta 14, based on Boncourt aerodrome, received a number (these included 160/17 and 198/17, dispatched from Schwerin on 24 December, and 183/17 on 2 January). The other units (Jasta 13, 15 and 19) do not seem to have received triplanes until they became components of JG II, and bulk consignments of triplanes from Schwerin to AFP VII for equipping Jagdstaffeln of JG II started in January (10 January – 162/17, 186/17, 215/17, 216/17, 218/17, 401/17; 21 January – 400/17, 405/17, 410/17, 412/17; 22 January – 170/17, 171/17, 200/17, 417/17, 419/17, 428/17; 24 January – 167/17, 202/17, 219/17, 402/17, 406/17, 415/17, 429/17).

JG II's formation date was 2 February 1918 and Hauptmann (Captain) Adolf Ritter von Tutschek was named as Kommandeur. Tutschek had spent some weeks assigned to GHQ while recovering from a serious shoulder wound received on 11 August 1917, following his 22nd victory. During this time he had been engaged in the appraisal of fighter aircraft types and tactics. He was thus aware of the intended formation of JG II and on learning that he was to receive this command, he understandably wanted his old Jasta 12, then based on Roucourt aerodrome, south of Douai in the II Armee area, to be one of the components of his formation. This meant that Jasta 12 would replace one of the previously selected Jagdstaffeln, and it was Jasta 14, despite its early receipt of triplanes, that was relegated and did not become part of JG II. By early March the component Jagdstaffeln were all based within some 10km to the south and south-east of Marle, and each had received a number of triplanes, although none had been equipped completely with the new type. Their aerodromes were as follows: Jasta 12, Toulis; Jasta 13, Reneuil-Ferme; Jasta 15, Autremencourt; and Jasta 19, Cuirieux.

Tutschek and his JG II Staff attached themselves to Jasta 12 at Toulis and he immediately started flying the triplane. His letters show how pleased he was with the aircraft: '. . . a quite fine machine, extremely manoeuvrable and climbs splendidly . . . really outstanding aircraft, just made for air-fighting . . .' However, his enthusiasm was to be short-lived. On 15 March, flying alone, he was shot down and killed in 404/17 near Brancourt. Vizefeldwebel (acting Sergeant-Major) Bannert collected Tutschek's body and noted that his white cloth, used for wiping his goggles, was still knotted through a button-hole of his flying-suit and tucked under the right-hand strap of his shoulder harness, indicating that it had not been used and that Tutschek had been the victim of a surprise attack.

90. Leutnant Emil Koch (left), Staffelfuehrer of Jasta 32b, and his OzbV, Leutnant Freiherr von Hunoldstein, pose with two blue-nosed Jasta 36 triplanes on Guesnain aerodrome, March 1918. No doubt they examined these aircraft from the nearby base of JG III at Erchin with envy, comparing them with their own unit's rather mediocre Pfalz D IIIa's. Both triplanes have the high-located circular access panels on the forward fuselages already mentioned, while the auxiliary bracing struts of the undercarriage axle wing fairing on the nearest aircraft can clearly be seen. This machine is 220/17 (Works No 1939) which was accepted at Schwerin on 16 January 1918, and displays the tailplane cross commented on in the previous caption.

▲90

91. Another triplane flown by Leutnant Bongartz in Jasta 36 was 512/17 (Works No 2139), seen immediately after arrival. The modifications to triplanes in this unit already mentioned have yet to be made. The aircraft still bears the works serial number and wing number chalked on all the wings near the wingtips and on the ailerons; in the original photograph these can be seen as 2139 and 1133 respectively. Components were marked in this way when an aircraft was dismantled for transport to facilitate reassembly at the AFP. Since the machine had been test-flown on acceptance at Schwerin, it merely required assembly without disturbing any of the settings previously determined to ensure that it would fly satisfactorily.

▲91

92. During the advance which resulted from the Spring Offensive, JG I occupied the British aerodrome at Léchelle on the evening of 26 March. This photograph of Jasta 6 triplanes lined up there was probably taken a few days later and shows the aircraft undergoing national insignia changes. The machine on the right appears to be 595/17 (Works No 2265), flown by Leutnant Franz Hemer, and bears part of his white wavy line marking, a symbol selected because of his wavy hair. The next aircraft was flown by Leutnant Robert Tuexen, marked with a thin black-bordered white fuselage band, and is believed to be 568/17 (Works No 2238). The fourth triplane in the line-up – thought to be 556/17 (Works No 2226) – is marked with a red fuselage band with a vertical wavy white line superimposed on it, which has been applied over a previously marked arrow-headed lightning flash. Previously flown by Leutnant Ludwig Beckmann, the fuselage band was in the colours of his native Westphalia.

▼92

93. Although Richthofen's combat report descriptions of 152/17 (Works No 1864) merely stated 'red top wing, red cowling, red wheels and red tail', this photograph reveals that all struts were painted red and the lack of camouflage streaking on the fuselage top decking between the tail unit and cockpit shows that this was also over-painted red. The forward limit of the red colour can be seen as a straight line across the decking immediately aft of the cockpit. Reflected light shows the original square white backgrounds on the top surface of the upper wing as a lighter shade of red; usually the fuselage crosses also revealed this feature, although it cannot be seen here. Whether or not this applied depended on the manner of over-painting to introduce the 5cm-wide white borders when the aircraft were first received.

94. Richthofen's all-red 425/17 (Works No 2009) at Léchelle in front of the Bessoneau hangars in late March 1918. From the protection around the engine and the use of a canvas propeller cover, it appears that the aircraft was not in current use at the time. It awaits the change of its iron cross national insignia to Balkenkreuze, which changes were actually being made to Jasta 11 triplanes on the aerodrome when this photograph was taken. Richthofen's then current all-red triplane was apparently 152/17, although he did not score any victories on it in that state of decoration. Note that the leading-edge protection fittings often visible on triplane wings (pressed hollow steel cups to keep the wings clear of the ground when they were placed on their leading-edges during storage) have been removed. These fittings often became detached in service and were not usually replaced. The distinctive inverted 'vee' blemish on the upper fuselage side fabric under the cockpit should be noted, since reference will be made to it in caption 116.

95. One of Richthofen's triplanes at Léchelle in late March apparently undergoing national insignia change to Balkenkreuze. Factory-applied stencilling under the centre-section of the top wing shows that this is almost certainly 477/17 (Works No 2103). The upper surface of the top wing of this aircraft was overpainted red, and the leading-edge of that surface shows this; interplane and centre-section struts, engine cowling and fabric wheel covers were also painted red. The tail was reportedly red, and this may have been on the upper surfaces only at this time, since the tailplane looks light underneath and the rear fuselage is not over-painted, the factory-applied under surface light blue being visible on the bottom left-hand longeron aft of the lifting handle. The rudder, which was probably previously painted red, has been over-painted white and its cross changed to meet the new requirements.

▲ 93

▲ 94 ▼ 95

▲ 96

96. Taken at Erchin in late March/early April, this photograph shows the thirteen triplanes received by Jasta 26 at that time. They are in the process of having the iron crosses of their national insignia converted to Balkenkreuze. Only the triplane on the left, flown by the Staffelfuehrer, Leutnant Fritz Loerzer, displays the black and white bands of the unit marking. This machine also had the top wing centre-section and the front third of its upper wing surface painted in black as a leader's

marking, and carried Loerzer's initials as a cast aluminium motif riveted to the front of the engine cowling. The lack of the black and white unit marking bands on the remaining machines (although a start has been made on two of them) shows that they have only just been delivered and indicates that at the opening of the Spring Offensive Jasta 26 was still equipped with its earlier Albatros D Vs.

97. Vizefeldwebel Otto Esswein of Jasta 26 poses with

his new triplane, 426/17 (Works No 2010), at Erchin in early April. This was shortly after the new machines had had their national insignia changed to Balkenkreuze and the black and white unit markings applied to rear fuselage and tail units. Some of the triplanes display pilot identification markings, but Esswein's large black initial letter 'E' has yet to be painted on the broad white fuselage band behind the cockpit, and this would also be marked on a white band across the centre of the top wing. The

distinctive, almost Chauvière shape (with its curved leading edge), of the Heine propeller without trademark transfer is in direct contrast to the symmetrical taper of the Axial propellers normally used on the triplane. The unusual practice in Jasta 26 of carrying the external rack for signal cartridges and mounting the signal pistol on the left-hand side of the fuselage should be noted.

▼ 97

The loss of Tutschek created a vacancy that was not easy to fill. It had been decided that the Kommandeur of a Jagdgeschwader had to be an 'active' (regular) officer, preferably with the rank of Hauptmann and an experienced and successful fighter pilot. Hauptmann Rudolf Berthold, the 27-victory Staffelfuehrer of Jasta 18, had previously asked Kogenluft for the command of a Jagdgeschwader for the coming offensive, but he had been severely wounded several times and was still recovering from his last wound, sustained on 10 October 1917. However, despite this disability, he was obviously highly suitable and was given the command of JG II; although during his convalescence Kogenluft personally expressly forbade him to fly.

The authority that Berthold was able to wield in having his own Jasta 18 replace one of the component Jagdstaffeln in JG II is considered to have been a previously unheard of procedure, yet there was a precedent – Tutschek had done exactly the same thing. However, in Tutschek's case JG II had not then been formed, while JG II was already a permanent formation. The only way that Berthold could get Jasta 18 into his new command was to change its number to that of one of the already established components in JG II, and that is what was done. Despite the manner of its execution, as outlined in the War Diaries of both Jasta 18 and Jasta 15, whereby listed personnel are shown to be transferred from one unit to the other, it was in fact a paper exercise that could be best described as 'for Jasta 18 read Jasta 15'. Thus it was merely a renumbering process and a complete interchange between these units took place. The only exception seems to have been the Jasta 15 Adjutant, Leutnant Monnington, who was retained by Berthold for a short time to smooth the entry of his previous Jasta into JG II. That Berthold wished to retain the Albatros D V, and not get involved in converting his stationary-engined pilots to the triplane at this critical time, is understandable – the offensive was about to open and Berthold wanted all component Jagdstaffeln of his Jagdgeschwader to remain fully operational.

The change of designations Jasta 15/18 took place on Guise aerodrome in the XVIII Armee area, whence JG II had moved on 19 March. The old Jasta 15 gave up the few triplanes it had on charge and moved to Bruille aerodrome, east of Douai in the XVII Armee area, where it was equipped with the Albatros D Va and Pfalz D IIIa. It was still considered to be a stationary-engined Jasta, as only a few pilots had actually converted to the triplane before the change mentioned took place. As a result, this unit did not obtain any operational successes

on the Fokker Dr I before relinquishing the type on leaving JG II.

During the offensive, JG II moved forward with XVIII Armee and by the end of March, when the advance ended, was based on the large aerodrome complex at Balâtre near Roye, which it shared with a number of Jagdstaffeln. The fact that some 150 fighters were operating from this location did not escape the notice of the enemy, and Balâtre was frequently bombed and shelled, causing JG II to lose 25 aircraft during the night of 12/13 April. A hurried move to Bonnieul-Ferme was made to recoup the losses, and the formation occupied Les Mesnil aerodrome near Nesle on 21 April. From there offensive operations were carried out in May and June to cover the right flank of the VII Armee during the advance towards Château-Thierry on the River Marne.

According to Hermann Becker, JG II seldom operated at full Jagdgeschwader strength, mainly because of the mixed nature of its equipment. The serviceability of its triplane Jagdstaffeln suffered because of the unreliability of the Oberursel engine, mostly due to the ever poorer quality of the lubricating oil, a factor which was compounded by increasing summer temperatures. Gradually Fokker D VIIs replaced the triplanes in JG II, but by mid-June Jasta 19 was only partially equipped and continued to use the triplane, while Jasta 12 had none of the new fighters and retained a full triplane complement. But in the offensive nature of the JG II commitment, the operational effectiveness of these two Jagdstaffeln was seriously reduced.

By now fuel was being rationed and each component Jasta in JG II was allocated only 14,000 litres (3,000 Imperial gallons) of petrol and 4,000 litres (900 Imperial gallons) of oil per month. The consumption of these precious commodities on triplane flying hours, that were far less productive than comparable time on the Fokker D VII, could not be allowed to continue, and on 24 June the Kofl of the XVIII Armee decreed that JG II's remaining triplanes should be taken out of service. Although this left some 40 per cent of the JG II pilots without aeroplanes to fly, the Fokker D VII supply situation was improving, and in anticipation of receiving the biplane fighter, the remaining triplanes of Jasta 19 and Jasta 12 were given up to AFP XVIII.

JAGDGESCHWADER III

In IV Armee the first indication that triplanes would re-equip Jagdstaffeln other than those in JG I was when Leutnant Walter von Buelow, Staffelfuehrer of Jasta 36, was invited to attend triplane test-flying at Adlershof

98. Ten triplanes of Jasta 11 lined up on Léchelle aerodrome in early April 1918, in front of the four Bessoneau hangars previously used by the R.E.8s of No 15 Squadron, RFC, flying for the V Corps of the British Third Army. The three Jasta 11 pilots in the foreground are (left to right): Unteroffizier Robert Eiserbeck (killed 12/4/18), Leutnant Hans Weiss (killed 2/5/18) and Vizefeldwebel Edgar Scholz (killed 2/5/18). Scholz is wearing the harness of the Heinecke parachute, the earliest operational examples having reached JG I in early March. This equipment was not immediately accepted by all the pilots until they learned of successful descents, or they themselves experienced a situation where a parachute would have been advantageous. Scholz was an early convert. Miraculously, he emerged unscathed from the remains of his triplane when, during a fierce dog-fight, an Albatros fighter falling out of control hit his machine and removed his tail unit, causing Scholz to spin several thousand metres to the ground. Eiserbeck had a similar harrowing experience when his control cables were shot through; after switching the engine off, his out-of-control arrival caused his triplane to somersault several times, but he was unharmed.

▲ 98

99. Leutnant Richard Wenzl's 588/17 (Works No 2258) at Léchelle, showing its black and white leading-edge markings. The aircraft next to it is believed to be Richthofen's red triplane, but since both 152/17 and 425/17 were painted in exactly the same way at that time, positive identification cannot be made. However, the presence of leading-edge protection fittings on the middle and lower wings suggest that this is in fact 152/17. The date is early April (Wenzl first arrived at Léchelle on 2 April) and the Balkenkreuze on both triplanes have just been applied and have cross arm ratios of approximately 1:3.

▲ 99   ▼ 100

100. This view of Wenzl's Jasta 11 triplane, 588/17, taken at the same time as the previous photograph, shows the standard JG I thick Balkenkreuze. While these are not as fat as those applied to triplanes of Jasta Boelcke, the cross bars are of a lower ratio than was intended and were later altered. Wenzl has applied his black and white fuselage band for personal identification. This was in the proportions of the ribbon of the Iron Cross decoration with the colours reversed, and was a marking that he had previously used in Jasta 31. Normal gunsights are fitted to both guns and this tends to confirm the date of the photograph. Wenzl used his left eye for aiming and adjusted his guns accordingly, which meant that he raised both sights on the left-hand gun and appears to have done this first on 5 April. The following day he made his first operational flight on the triplane under Richthofen.

early in November 1917, during his home leave. Since this coincided with the temporary grounding of all triplanes due to the wing problem, the proposed flying obviously did not take place. But doubtless von Buelow was then aware of the intention to form JG III in IV Armee, and on 13 December he became the Staffel-fuehrer of Jagdstaffel Boelcke. This unit was one of the most effective Jagdstaffeln at the front, ranking second only to Richthofen's Jasta 11 in terms of successful air combats. Originally formed as Jasta 2 under Haupt-mann Oswald Boelcke, the unit was honoured by Imperial decree to include the name of its first Staffel-fuehrer in its designation from 17 December 1916. It was certainly the first Jasta to be earmarked as a component of JG III and received its first Fokker D V, for transition training, on 1 January 1918. However, von Buelow was killed on 6 January, just before the first triplanes began to arrive at Jasta Boelcke.

By the end of January both Jasta Boelcke and Jasta 36 had a number of triplanes on strength, and although no details of the particular instances are available, it appears that some of their machines had been attacked by other German aircraft operating in the IV Armee area. Although the Sopwith Triplane was no longer opposed to IV Armee, experience during the summer of 1917 made some German units particularly allergic to aeroplanes of the triplane configuration. In an attempt to improve their recognition a few Jasta Boelcke triplanes were marked with national insignia on their tailplanes, but these were generally painted out when the unit marking was applied. However, the practice was more widespread in Jasta 36, and in that unit the tailplane display of national insignia almost became a unit marking in itself for a period.

On 2 February 1918, the formation date of JG III, both Jasta Boelcke and Jasta 36 were, as expected, included as component Jagdstaffeln. The other two Jagdstaffeln selected were Jasta 26 and Jasta 27, equipped with Albatros D Vs; but as they too were expected to receive the triplane, their pilots practised flying on Fokker D Vs while based at Bavichove (7km north-east of Courtrai), which location they shared with Jasta Boelcke. The Fokker D Vs were doubtless the same machines that had been used in January by Jasta Boelcke for the same purpose.

By mid-February the units occupied the following aerodromes, all in the vicinity of Courtrai: Jasta Boelcke, Marcke; Jasta 26, Marckebeeke; Jasta 27, Marckebeeke; and Jasta 36, Kuerne.

After Oberleutnant Bruno Loerzer, Staffelfuehrer of Jasta 26, was named as Kommandeur of JG III, his brother, Leutnant Fritz Loerzer, who had recently

formed Jasta 63, was given the command of Jasta 26 on 20 February. With only a month to go before the opening of the Spring Offensive, the need for triplanes in Jasta 26 and Jasta 27 was urgent, but due to the shortage of Fokker Dr Is, these units had to continue using their Albatros D Vs.

JG III was assigned to XVII Armee for the Spring Offensive and between 12 and 15 March moved to a large flat expanse of farmland east of the village of Erchin (some 10km south-east of Douai), which prov-ided a natural aerodrome. To preserve the secrecy of this concentration for the coming attack, it was forbidden to pitch hangar tents for the aeroplanes and the machines were dispersed in farm buildings in the area, sometimes being dismantled for this purpose. Flying activity was restricted to flights to familiarize the pilots with the surrounding terrain and even these were of low frequency. Hangar tents were pitched on the evening of 21 March after the offensive had begun.

A consignment of triplanes arrived in late March, just as the advance came to a halt. The exact number is not known, but there were too few for both Jasta 26 and Jasta 27. Jasta 26 was completely equipped and Jasta 27 received the remainder and as a result continued to operate at about half strength, with its Albatros D Vs to make up the established strength of fourteen aeroplanes.

After the advance ceased on 28 March, JG III had little time to reflect on the 30 victories it had gained during the offensive and between 12 and 17 April moved north to occupy the aerodrome at Halluin-Ost (some 10km south-west of Courtrai) in the IV Armee for the forthcoming Kemmel Offensive. When this attack com-menced on 25 April, as the infantry went over the top they were supported by low-flying two-seaters of sixteen Schlachtstaffeln, which were protected by ten Jagd-staffeln in two Jagdgruppen, while JG III reigned supreme in the upper airspace. The British were overwhelmed, and during the first day of the offensive the Germans established aerial supremacy not only over the fighting area but well behind enemy lines.

When the offensive fighting ceased on 1 May, JG III had some respite and during the following three weeks began to receive the new Fokker D VII biplane fighter. Some of the first went to Jasta 27 and for a period this unit was operating three types: Albatros D V, Fokker Dr I and Fokker D VII. Other Fokker D VIIs went to Jasta Boelcke and Jasta 26. These units had given up many of their triplanes to AFP IV, before continuing the nomadic existence expected of a Jagdgeschwader; between 21 and 24 May, JG III moved south to the scene of the next offensive when, assigned to VII Armee, it occupied Vivaise aerodrome, some 10km north-west of Lâon.

▲101

101. Still with Jasta 11 when photographed at Foucaucourt in April, 146/17 now has the rear fuselage, tailplane and elevators over-painted and a fuselage band added for pilot identification. The interplane and centre-section struts have meanwhile received the red Jasta 11 identifying colour, and the national insignia have been changed to Balkenkreuze to meet the March Idflieg instruction. These are typical of the over-thick type that resulted either from hurried alteration or the receipt of incomplete instructions.

102. Fokker triplane 195/17 (Work No 1913) flown by Leutnant Hermann Vallendor of Jasta Boelcke, early April 1918. This machine was one of a small number of triplanes powered by the engine made by the Rhenania – Motorenfabrik AG of Mannheim (Rhemag) which was known as the Oberursel UR II (Rh). The national insignia are the newly marked Balkenkreuze, the arms of which have a very low width-to-length ratio (1:2.5) and were later modified to a higher value to improve cross recognition. The smudged appearance of the fuselage cross suggests either the use of a paint that was not fast, or use of the aircraft before the paint had dried following cross alteration. Observe how the white 'V' marking on the fuselage side is dirty and discoloured compared with the more recent white of the cross borders. Note that the undercarriage axle wing fairing has been reinforced by an external spanwise member to support the two auxiliary struts.

▼102

103. In this line-up of nine Jasta Boelcke triplanes on Halluin-Ost aerodrome in April 1918, all aircraft bear the thick cross bars of low ratio in their national insignia which were later modified on rudders and fuselages. The two aircraft nearest the camera show the unit marking of black and white tailplanes, elevators and rear fuselages with the colours reversed, possibly for Kette identification. Kempf's machine, although carrying the same wing inscriptions as 213/17, is a different aeroplane (see next caption). The third aircraft in the line-up is Bolle's machine, which is shown at a slightly later date in a subsequent photograph.

104. Apart from the reversed tail colours and the changed national insignia, comparison of the camouflage streaking and wing inscriptions with 213/17 show that this is not the same aeroplane. It is probably 493/17 (Works No 2120), a machine that Kempf is known to have flown, using it to score his fourth and final victory on 8 May.

105. Leutnant Walter Goettsch, Staffelfuehrer of Jasta 19, sitting in 419/17 (Works No 2003) which would later have the top surface of the upper mainplane over-painted white. The duplicated centre-section bracing wires were fitted to only a few triplanes, and 419/17 is the only machine in Jasta 19 known to have had them. Note how the lower lengths of the cables, below the turnbuckles, are encased in streamline-section tubes, taped together at their intersection to reduce their amplitude of vibration.

106. Goettsch's triplane, 419/17, undergoing rectification of what appears to have been a major defect, one which obviously could not be accomplished by access via the opened bottom tray panel under the forward fuselage, since the centre-section bracing wires have been disconnected to take off the top panel fairing, and the guns, already removed, are seen under the starboard bottom wing. The photographer behind the port wings of the triplane was probably one of a team responsible for the series of official Kogenluft photographs taken at this time on Balâtre aerodrome. The mechanic at the wingtip of the Siemens D III looks like a painter and has probably just altered the iron cross national insignia of this aircraft on the wings and rudder, there being no need to change the fuselage cross since this was deleted in Jasta 19. In any case, on this aircraft the whole plywood fuselage tailplane and fin would be over-painted white, the machine being intended for the use of Leutnant Goettsch.

107. To allow the mechanic on the step-ladder easier access to what appears to be the fuel tank area, his helpers have raised the tail via the lifting handles, so providing a good view of the top wing cross location and the white swastika marking on the fuselage. The top fairing panel has been removed (visible on the ground at the right), revealing the unpainted square-ribbed reinforcement (with powder stains on its leading-edge) between the aperture for the fuel tank filler neck and the streamlined fairing of the fuel contents gauge, to lessen blast damage from the left-hand gun. The streamlined tube fairings for the centre-section bracing cables rest on the starboard middle wing, while the disconnected duplicated turnbuckles hang down in the centre-section. If the problem was a leaking fuel tank, this was extremely difficult to repair and may have entailed a tank change, necessitating the considerable dismantling shown. Goettsch was killed on 10 April flying this aeroplane, when he brought down an R.E.8 near Gentelles as his 20th victory. During the final stage of this action, when he was flying at low altitude behind the British lines, he was presumably hit by ground fire and his machine was observed to slip out of a right-hand turn into a steep dive and burst into flames on hitting the ground.

▲105

▲106 ▼107

The attack against the French opened on 27 May in the Battle of Chemin des Dames. The break-through was complete, and in continuous advance the River Marne near Château-Thierry was reached on 31 May. The rapid progress meant that JG III had to move forward to new aerodromes. Jasta Boelcke and Jasta 36 were on Epitaph-Ferme on 6 June, and Jasta 27 and Jasta 26 occupied the aerodrome at Mont de Soissons Ferme on 3 and 8 June respectively.

Gradually more Fokker D VIIs became available and by mid-June most of the triplanes of Jasta Boelcke, Jasta 26 and Jasta 27 had been relinquished to AFP VII.

Not all the component Jagdstaffeln in JG III were completely equipped with the Fokker D VII and triplanes remained in small numbers. Jasta 36 retained the triplane longest and when it moved to Vauxéré on 19 July was still operating the type. Generally the few triplanes still with JG III's other Jagdstaffeln were retained only as reserve aircraft. The problems that affected JG II triplane operations were also applicable to JG III and fuel and oil rationing, as well as summer temperatures, meant that the triplanes were no longer effective fighters and they were replaced as rapidly as Fokker D VII availability allowed.

NON-JAGDGESCHWADER USE

RECORDS of types and numbers of aircraft used by the 81 Jagdstaffeln are at best fragmentary, and as far as can be ascertained the triplane was only operated in quantity by three Jagdstaffeln that were not component units of a Jagdgeschwader. These were Jasta 14, Jasta 5 and Jasta 34b. The latter two units used ex-JG I aircraft from May onwards when the type was being replaced in JG I by the Fokker D VII. Thus Jasta 14 was the only non-Jagdgeschwader Jagdstaffel to use the triplane in quantity during the period from January to April 1918 when the type was seen as first-line Jagdgeschwader equipment.

Towards the end of 1917 the most successful Jagd-staffel in VII Armee was Jasta 15 which, as mentioned previously, was the unit selected to introduce the triplane into VII Armee. There is no doubt that the efficiency of Jasta 15 stemmed from its Staffelfuehrer, who had been responsible for more than half of the successful air combats credited to the unit. However, as regards re-equipment with triplanes, the loss of Gonter-mann obviously changed the emphasis from Jasta 15 to the next most effective Jagdstaffel in VII Armee. This was Leutnant Hans Werner's Jasta 14, recently trans-ferred from V Armee, now based on Boncourt aero-drome (7km north-east of Sissonne), and it received triplanes in January 1918.

That Jasta 14 did not, in fact, become a component unit of JG II has already been mentioned. Its early equipment with triplanes obviously made it eligible for JG II and, one would suspect, a much more suitable unit at that time than either Jasta 13, 15 or 19; so there must have been some other reason for its exclusion when Tutschek wanted to include his old Jasta 12 in JG II. It is possible that there was a personality clash between

Werner and Tutschek. Such happenings were not uncommon; they received careful consideration by Kogenluft and were often accommodated.

However, what is even more surprising is that Jasta 14 was allowed to retain its triplanes when there were too few of these aircraft fully to equip Jagdstaffeln in JG I–III. Perhaps Werner had to fight to keep the triplanes; as events show, he was certainly reluctant to give them up, and Jasta 14 probably still had a few on its strength until the end of August 1918. A full complement of triplanes was never maintained in Jasta 14. Initially a number of Albatros D Va's were used until May, to make up a reasonable strength, and after that date Fokker D VIIs were used in the same capacity. An establishment of fourteen aircraft was something that few units achieved in 1918, and in Jasta 14 an average figure would appear to have been about ten, half of them triplanes.

Assigned to XVII Armee for the Spring Offensive, Jasta 14 occupied Masny aerodrome north of Erchin on 19 March. After obtaining a few victories in the fighting that accompanied the advance, the unit moved on 11 April to VI Armee, being based on Phalempin aero-drome, some 10km south of Lille, in readiness for the Kemmel Offensive. Jasta 14 was to remain on this aerodrome, which it shared with Jasta 30, until 18 August, before being forced to leave due to enemy shelling, when it moved to Faches near Lille. During the four months of its operations from Phalempin, the unit obtained twelve victories over British opponents, mostly S.E.5a's. Losses during this period were three pilots: one killed in a flying accident, one died of wounds and one PoW.

Although it is not confirmed that Jasta 14 was a

▲108

108. Leutnant Rudolf Rienau of Jasta 19 with his white-striped 504/17 (Works No 2131). In this unit the triplane fuselage crosses were over-painted so that the national insignia did not conflict with the pilots' personal identification markings. This was done in a meticulous manner that closely resembled

▼109

the original Fokker greenish-brown camouflage application, as can clearly be seen here. Rienau, who eventually became the Staffelfuehrer of Jasta 19, survived the war and was credited with 6 victories. He remained in aviation and became a flying instructor. He was killed in a flying accident at Staaken aerodrome near

Berlin on 23 May 1925.

109. Leutnant Rienau's mechanics pose for the Kogenluft photographer at Balâtre with 504/17. When the white fuselage striping was originally applied, this machine was marked with iron cross type national insignia. Now, in common with the other Jasta 19

triplanes, these have been changed to Balkenkreuze. Note the thin dark-coloured spanwise stripes on wing leading-edges as a dividing line between the top surface camouflage and the light-blue under surface colours, a feature not seen on early production triplanes.

component of Jagdgruppe 7 (Jasta 29, 30, 43 and 52), it flew with this formation and is included with these units from 6 August, when its designation was changed to Jagdgruppe A.

Extracts from the personal diary of Josef Raesch (a Fokker D VII pilot in Jasta 43) show the continued involvement of Jasta 14 triplanes on flying operations during June and July:

24 June: 'We took off together with Leutnant Werner's triplane Staffel. However, we only managed to assemble 14 aeroplanes (6 triplanes). Jasta 14 is the only Staffel that will not part with the triplane. The machine is more manoeuvrable than the D VII, but can only climb to about 4,800 metres.'

27 June: '. . . joined up again with Jasta 14 triplanes . . .'

1 July: '. . . join Staffel 14 triplanes on the way to the front . . .'

2 July: '. . . also Staffel 14 flies with us . . . I remain with two triplanes at our old height . . .

Raesch relates that on 9 July during a fight between six Fokker D VIIs of Jasta 43 and thirteen de Havillands, triplanes of Jasta 14 joined in the combat, and how on 17 July he was joined in the air by four triplanes of Jasta 14. Finally he mentions that Jasta 43 maintained contact with Jasta 14 which was also in the air with its triplanes on 22 July. It is significant that further references to Jasta 14 do not mention triplanes specifically, indicating that Jasta 14 was by then probably beginning to use a higher proportion of Fokker D VIIs in its formations.

However, a British War Diary entry of '5 triplanes seen on 19 August between Laventie and Haubourin' refers almost certainly to aircraft from Jasta 14, since the location given is only some 15km west of Faches. But the triplane's time was running out, even in Jasta 14, and they seem to have disappeared from the unit's roster at about that time. Certainly by 30 September, when Jasta 14 left Faches aerodrome to become a component of IV Armee Jagdgruppe 3 under Oberleutnant Auffahrt (Jasta 14, 16b, 29 and 56), based at Cruyshoutem, it was entirely Fokker D VII-equipped.

During the Spring Offensive Jasta 5 and Jasta 46 comprised Jagdgruppe 2 and from 17 April were based at Cappy. Jasta 5 was thus ideally located to receive ex-JG I triplanes to replace its Albatros D Va's when Jasta 6 and Jasta 11 began to receive Fokker D VIIs in early May. A full complement was received, but the triplanes were considered to be merely stop-gap equipment until Jasta 5 itself could obtain Fokker D VIIs. The triplanes were used with success during May and June and were gradually replaced with Fokker D VIIs. It is believed that by the time Jasta 5 moved from Cappy to Moislains

on 4 August, few, if any, triplanes were on its strength

The Bavarian Jasta 34b, based at Foucaucourt (some 5km south of Cappy), received a number of ex-JG I triplanes early in May. According to Rudolf Stark, there was great excitement when the triplanes arrived, and they were looked upon as superior to the Albatros D Va and Pfalz D IIIa with which the unit was then equipped. However, engine trouble in a variety of forms did not engender a successful association for Jasta 34b with the triplane. Logbook entries made by the Staffelfuehrer, Oberleutnant Robert Greim, contain a tale of woe about 'blued' and lost cylinders; but he also records that on 3 June a four-strong triplane patrol was flown, this being repeated five days later. The obvious attention that was lavished on the triplane appears to have been transferred to the few Fokker D VIIs that arrived on 15 June. The following day Jasta 34b was able to make what Greim describes as a 'Geschwaderstart' (squadron take-off), when a patrol was carried out with three Fokker D VIIs and three triplanes. This unit continued to operate its original equipment during this period, and the engine problems with the triplanes caused them to take a back seat, especially with the arrival of more Fokker D VIIs. The triplanes were probably little used by Jasta 34b after the end of June.

In most cases the triplane lingered on in some units, only because there were insufficient Fokker D VIIs to go around. A few pilots (usually Staffelfuehrer) managed to obtain a triplane for their personal use long after the type had ceased to be effective unit equipment. Some pilots preferred the triplane for low-altitude work where its manoeuvrability was better than that of the Fokker D VII, and it was used, for example, in attacks against observation balloons. One Staffelfuehrer who used the triplane to good effect was Leutnant Josef Jacobs of Jasta 7; his initial experience with the type had been punctuated with engine trouble, a problem he eventually solved by using captured Allied rotary engines. On 24 March, his personal diary records: '. . . made a third flight with my triplane. It is much slower at height than the Albatros D Va and only of little use. At low level, it is very manoeuvrable and equal to the British machines'.

Jacobs, who led the Albatros D Va's and later the Fokker D VIIs of Jasta 7 in his triplane, all of the aircraft painted black, became well known on the British front. He had a long and successful career on the triplane, alternating between it and his Fokker D VII. He could obviously select the triplane for work when the weather conditions favoured its performance, and from the number of victory claims he submitted in the last few months of the war, it is apparent that his higher-

▲110

110. Leutnant Hans Koerner of Jasta 19 with his white zigzag-marked triplane 503/17 (Works No 2130). The Oigee telescopic sight is centrally mounted on two tubes bolted to the slotted air-cooled mantels of the LMG 08/15 machine-guns. To facilitate its use Koerner has removed the normal gun butt protective padding and fitted a

central chin-rest. He has also dispensed with the usual plain vee backsight on the right-hand gun and replaced it with a small circular backsight. Koerner, who came to Jasta 19 from Jasta 8 at Leutnant Goettsch's request, survived the war and was credited with 6 victories. He remained in aviation, but lost his life on a motor-cycle

journey to his aerodrome (date and place not known).

111. This colourful line-up of eleven Jasta 19 triplanes at Balâtre near Roye includes Goettsch's 419/17 (second aircraft from right), which was lost on 10 April. On the extreme left is one of two Siemens D IIIs which arrived on 4 April; it is

still marked with the iron cross national insignia. The date of this official Kogenluft photograph is thus defined as being between these dates. The rear of the original photograph was dated 19 April, but this was obviously the date of print processing by the Stabsbildabteilung (Staff photo section) of the XVIII Armee.

▼111

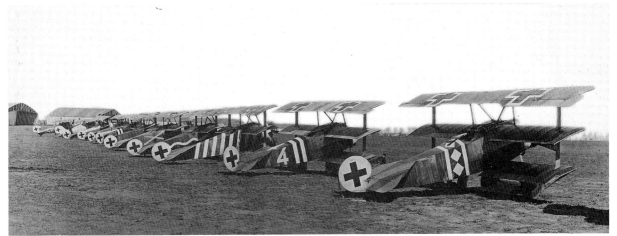

112. Some different Jasta 19 machines are shown in this later Balâtre line-up of nine triplanes, while at the extreme left can be seen the white-fuselage Siemens D III (which was already in this state of decoration at the time of the previous photograph) and the previously seen Siemens D III, its rudder cross now of Balkenkreuz type. It is possible that this official photograph was taken after the loss of Goettsch, and shows Leutnant Arthur Rahn's 433/17 (Works No 2058) nearest the camera

with a deputy leader's streamer on its rudder. However, the shadow on the extreme right suggests the presence of another aircraft, which has been omitted from the photograph; this may have been the Goettsch triplane. The date could have been 10–12 April. Some of the triplanes shown in either or both of these photographs were destroyed during the night of 12/13 April when Balâtre came under fire from French long-range guns and some 200 high-explosive shells hit the aerodrome, setting

fire to a large hangar and causing JG II to lose 25 aircraft. As a result, Jasta 19 left Balâtre on 13 April for Bonneuil-Ferme south of Ham to escape the attentions of the French artillery.

113. Jasta 12 triplanes on Balâtre aerodrome, early April 1918. Blumenbach's 217/17, at left, clearly shows the additional white fuselage band that this triplane carried, a part of the marking which is usually obscured in other photographs of this aircraft. Neckel's white

chevron-marked triplane can be seen in the right background. These three triplanes all display 'thin' crosses and, as explained in the text, have reverted to the use of white rudders following the implementation of the 17 March Kogenluft directive. The painter responsible for the nearest machine has even gone a stage further, as can be seen, although this rudder may have been a replacement component. Note that this triplane has had its engine and cowling removed.

▲114

114. Fokker triplane 581/17 (Works No 2251) reached the front in April 1918 and in common with all Fokker Dr Is displayed completely out-of-date national insignia on arrival. The manufacturer's plate riveted to the right-hand side of the engine cowling can clearly be seen. Note the right-hand shoulder strap of the safety harness, a necessity in a fighter capable of violent

manoeuvres. Although this was a standard fitting on all triplanes, some pilots did not like the restraint that it provided and replaced it with a simple lap-strap. The wheels have been fitted 'outside-in' which, in addition to improving ground handling, allowed easier access to the tyre inflation valve. This machine later fell into French hands and was restored to flying condition

after the war, then being fitted with a Nieuport's engine, cowling and propeller.

115. The port side cockpit coaming on 581/17 has been removed better to illuminate the compass Steuertabelle (deviation card), which is glued to the rear of the aluminium ammunition box. The Bamberg or Pfadfinder (pathfinder) compass was

situated almost at floor level between the pilot's seat and the starboard fuselage side, being supported in a gimbal mounting. On the aerodrome, away from any disturbing influence, the aeroplane was placed in flying position on different known magnetic headings and the compass read. Comparison of these indications/headings showed the amount of magnetic deviation caused by the aircraft's structure. This was offset by placing small corrector magnets into slots in the mounting below the compass. It was impossible to remove all deviation; that remaining was entered into the Steuertabelle and this showed the pilot what compass heading was necessary to ensure that the aircraft was steered in the required direction. The card on 581/17 showed that its compass was swung at Schwerin on 24 March 1918. The instrument between the guns is the Maximall fuel contents gauge, its pointer operated by a float unit in the tank. The lack of an instrument panel should be noted; the object on the left cockpit wall is the Bosch engine ignition switch.

▼115

powered triplanes (he had two most of the time) which used 120hp Clerget engines, were potent instruments, especially when operated at low altitude.

But in general the triplane's days were over. It had become almost a curiosity, and the few that were still in the front-line area in November 1918 were either destroyed during the retreat or left to rot – the Allies did not want them either, the victor's demands being focused on the triplane's successor, the Fokker D VII.

RICHTHOFEN'S TRIPLANES

CONTRARY to popular belief, Richthofen did not fly special machines. His triplanes were standard production aircraft and were not equipped in any particular way for his use. He was much too fine a leader of fighting airmen to use his rank or position to obtain weapons that were superior to those that his men used. The aeroplanes were shipped from the factory, as were all other Fokker Dr I triplanes, in the basic Fokker camouflage scheme adopted for the type and only received the red colouring associated with Richthofen when they came on the strength of his front-line fighting formation, Jagdstaffel 11, to which component of Jagdgeschwader I Richthofen understandably attached himself.

The serial numbers and brief descriptions of the markings carried for identification – taken from Richthofen's combat reports – only tell us about the aircraft flown in the respective successful combats. He doubtless flew other Fokker triplanes without scoring victories on them, and since in those cases combat reports (if submitted) are not available, the identities of such aircraft remain unknown. Documentation shows that he flew the following machines:

102/17 (victories Nos 60 and 61, September 1917)
114/17 (written off in emergency landing at Zilverberg, 30 October 1917)
127/17 (victories Nos 71, 74 and 76, March/April 1918)
152/17 (victories Nos 64, 65 and 66, March 1918)
161/17 (visit to Jasta 5 at Boistrancourt, March 1918)
425/17 (victories Nos 79 and 80, April 1918. Killed in this machine)
477/17 (victories Nos 67, 68, 69, 70, 72, 73, 75, 77 and 78, March/April 1918)
525/17 (visit to Jasta 5 at Boistrancourt, 17 March 1918)

Contemporary war correspondents have stated that Richthofen's reserve aircraft had red wings and that from the beginning of the March Offensive his regular machine was over-painted completely red. It is known from Richthofen's combat report descriptions that 425/17 was painted red on 20 April. This machine was not new, having been accepted on 8 January 1918, and had, prior to the offensive which started on 21 March, presumably been initially marked in the same manner as his other triplanes. These aircraft were 127/17, 152/17 and 477/17 and they all had the top surface of the upper wing, tail unit, engine cowling and undercarriage wheels painted red. It is known that the last recorded dates of Richthofen's combat use of 127/17 and 477/17 were 6 April and 7 April respectively, and that on those occasions the aircraft had only the partial red colouring mentioned. It would therefore appear that these machines were in fact Richthofen's reserve triplanes. (The war correspondents' mention that the reserve aircraft had red wings was an over-simplification, but obviously sufficed for them to differentiate between the reserve aircraft and Richthofen's regular all-red machine.)

When 152/17 was preserved in the Berlin Zeughaus museum it was painted completely red. Since it is known that when Richthofen obtained his 66th victory in it on 18 March this aircraft bore only partial red decoration, it was obviously over-painted red after this date, which was still a few days before the beginning of the offensive. Doubtless this machine was at that time seen as his regular aircraft (see chapter on 'Museum Pieces').

The manner in which his various triplanes were painted – with the top surface of the upper wing, engine cowling and tail unit in red – provided an almost completely red aircraft when viewed from above, which was the position from which identification was required when leading his formation – i.e., as leader he was out in front and lower than the other machines. No photographs of 127/17 and 425/17 with the partial red decoration have been seen, and only one of 477/17 in this condition. It can thus be assumed that these aircraft were painted in a similar manner to 152/17, and that they also sported a red fuselage top decking from the tail unit to the cockpit (which is clearly visible in the photograph of 152/17); this is a style of colour/marking exposure known to have been favoured in Jagdgeschwader I and it further enhanced the top surface display. However, there is no doubt that in the partial

▲116

116. Richthofen's red-painted 425/17 seen in its final state of decoration shortly before he was brought down and killed in this triplane. The narrow chord (15cm wide) of the national insignia cross bars on the now white rudder and on the fuselage have been changed from the thicker type (25cm wide) of Balkenkreuze that resulted from quickly changing iron cross insignia as explained in the text. The picture is believed to have been taken on Belle Aise Ferme aerodrome when Richthofen visited the two-seater unit Flieger Abteilung (A) 227, whose disciplinary Feldwebel (sergeant-major), standing by the cockpit, has placed two guards on the Rittmeister's (cavalry captain) famous aeroplane. The blemish on the fuselage fabric below the cockpit (a small inverted 'vee') shows that this is the same machine depicted earlier (94) with iron cross markings at Léchelle.

117. This photograph of Richthofen talking to Leutnant Loewenhardt and playing with his dog Moritz was taken at Cappy on 21 April 1918 by Leutnant Wenzl, a few minutes before Richthofen took off on his last flight. The white-tailed triplane in the background is a new machine recently arrived for Jagdstaffel 4, which received its first triplanes the previous day. Although the off-white unit marking has been applied to engine cowling, interplane struts and fabric wheel covers, the national insignia has yet to be changed to Balkenkreuze.

▼117

red schemes used on Richthofen's triplanes, which emphasized the upper surfaces, the under surfaces of the tail unit were also included, since he himself considered that individual aircraft should be so marked to identify a pilot within a formation. To quote Richthofen: '. . . within the Staffel everyone has his special marking on the machine, the best place for this is on the rear part of the tail, top and bottom'. On a machine with a complete Jagdstaffel 11 colour scheme, the interplane, centre-section and undercarriage struts were also painted red; however, photographic evidence shows that this was not always done.

As already mentioned, from the beginning of the March Offensive, Richthofen had his aeroplane painted completely red. It is known that he had done this previously in 1917 when his Albatros D V had also been completely over-painted red, and it is interesting to consider the reason for this. Richthofen was a great admirer of the ground fighting troops, especially the infantry, and one of his most prized possessions was his famous knotted walking stick, a gift from some Unter-offiziere (corporals) who had carved it while under enemy fire in the front-line trenches. It was to reaffirm this bond with the ordinary soldiers that he extended the red colour of his aircraft to include all the under surfaces as well, in order to make his machine more easily recognizable to those who saw him in action, and so bolster their morale. He related his feelings in this regard to his mother during his home leave in September 1917, when he was recovering from his head wound. His mother had asked him to be a little more friendly than he had been to the frequent callers and well-wishers. He replied brusquely and told her that he did not care what his public at home thought; it was what the German soldiers in the field felt that mattered, saying: 'Something exults within me when I fly over our trenches and see the soldiers rejoice when they recognize me. There is a jubilation in their tired, grey, hungry faces that you should see, as they jump out of cover, often exposing themselves to danger, waving up to me with their rifles – that is my reward, mother, my finest reward.'

Red was not an easily available colour and was not held in stores by units in the field, unlike black and white and certain camouflage colours which were required for finishing aircraft after repair or during national insignia changes. Its shortage was such that Richthofen often dispatched his Werkmeister, Josef Holzapfel, to search out sources of red (and other) paint in the rear areas. This was done using a two-seat aircraft, and on all such non-operational flights the aircraft's occupants had to carry a document of flight authorization, signed by a superior officer, stating the destination and purpose of the flight. Because there was no telling where the hunt for the paint would end, Richthofen gave Holzapfel a blank authorization form bearing his signature. This unusual procedure often resulted in aerodrome authorities doubting the correctness of Holzapfel's orders, and having to telephone Richthofen to verify the authenticity of the flight authorization. Such a practice back-fired on Holzapfel on one occasion when he took advantage of the enticing position that he found himself in. After obtaining the necessary paint at Lille, instead of returning to base he flew on to Brussels to have a night out. Richthofen, who had been informed by the aerodrome duty officer at Brussels of the over-nighting two-seater with the 'doubtful' document bearing his signature, did not admonish Holzapfel on his return. His off-hand question asking Holzapfel if he had enjoyed himself in Brussels showed the Werkmeister that Richthofen was aware of his misdemeanour. Holzapfel did not attempt to find any excuse, which satisfied Richthofen, and also ensured that there was no further misuse of privilege.

Since the red colour came from a variety of sources (captured Allied red dope was doubtless also used), the exact colour and shade obviously varied to quite a degree. Because the triplane used a linseed oil protective varnish finish, ordinary oil paint, suitably thinned, could be used without causing any interaction with the cellulose dope.

The choice of red stemmed from the use of reddish-brown as a camouflage colour on wings and tails in late 1916 and early 1917, but extending this colour to the varnished plywood fuselages of Albatros fighters at the time showed that, far from being a good camouflage colour on this component, it actually made the aircraft more easily visible at long ranges. This property was turned to good effect in the adoption of markings to enable individual pilots to be identified; it was more effective than the use of a personal symbol and was especially favoured by formation leaders. (The ineffectiveness of reddish-brown as an upper surface camouflage colour was recognized by Idflieg, which issued an order prohibiting its use on new production aircraft from 12 April 1917.)

Another aspect that promoted the use of this colour as a front-line marking was the ready identification of a machine that had been engaged in a successful air combat. Fights were followed by flak batteries and by special Luftschutz Offiziere (air defence officers), and it was often the mention of a specific colour or marking in their reports that provided the corroboration that Kogenluft required for confirmation of victories claimed by the pilots. This use of red was fostered by Jagdstaffel

▲118

▲119 ▼120

118. Leutnant Steinhaeuser (left) and Leutnant Wenzl with 588/17 at Cappy in late April. The previously mentioned alteration to the gunsights can be seen, both foresight and backsight of the left-hand gun being raised on small pillars to suit Wenzl's aiming taste. Although the rudder cross is not visible, this would certainly be of the same proportions as the fuselage cross, now updated, the width to length of the cross arms in the 1:4 ratio originally called for. The width of the white surrounding border has been increased to 10cm and is thus still narrower than laid down, but this form of altered cross was now common to all Jasta 11 triplanes. Because the fuselage band covered the military number, it was usual in Jasta 11 to re-mark the serial in the vicinity of the left-hand fuselage national insignia; on this aeroplane, 588 was painted on the fabric between the fuselage band and the lower white border of the vertical cross bar. Note that the wing crosses remain as applied at Léchelle in the original conversion to Balkenkreuze from the iron crosses.

119. Leutnant Werner Steinhaeuser of Jasta 11 with 564/17 (Works No 2234) which was another of the Rhemag Oberursel UR II (Rh) powered triplanes. The photograph was taken at Cappy in late April by Leutnant Wenzl and shows an aeroplane which is only a few weeks old since 564/17 was accepted at Schwerin as recently as 6 April. This triplane also had a re-marked military serial number in exactly the same location as Wenzl's machine. Steinhaeuser's individual markings are the striped tailplane and elevators and the fuselage band bearing a diagonal cross, which insignia was repeated on the fuselage decking. The colours were apparently those of his old regiment, Feld-Artillerie Regiment Nr 61 (2 Grossherzog von Hessen), and are thought to have been red on a golden yellow background. The step for cockpit entry was on the port side on the triplane and explains the use of the left-hand bottom wing as the best place to keep flying clothing and Heinecke harnesses for pilots at immediate readiness, as used above by Steinhaeuser and Wenzl.

120. Also taken by Leutnant Wenzl at the end of April at Cappy, this photograph was inscribed by Wenzl as 'Weiss, mein Kamerad und Begleiter' (Weiss, my comrade and guide), and shows Leutnant Hans Weiss, Kettenfuehrer (Flight leader) of Jasta 11, in front of his triplane. Although reportedly flying a white triplane, a colour adopted for personal identification because of his name (weiss – white), his aircraft was not completely over-painted white, but had this colour applied to the upper surface of the top wing, rear fuselage and tail unit and on the fuselage decking from the cockpit aft. This was a colour display common in JG I for a formation leader, and when viewed from above would cause Weiss's triplane to appear predominantly white. All struts, fabric wheel covers and engine cowling were painted in red, the identifying colour of Jasta 11. There is no doubt that this aeroplane is 545/17 (Works No 2213), the machine that Weiss was flying on 2 May 1918 when he was shot down and killed.

121. The original Jasta 15 had been compelled to give up its triplanes when it was redesignated Jasta 18 and left JG II. However, the triplanes had been popular with the pilots, and although now flying Albatros D Va's and Pfalz D IIIs they still hoped for triplane equipment: But it would seem that only the Staffelfuehrer, Leutnant August Raben, was successful: he managed to acquire 479/17 (Works No 2105) for his personal use. The Jasta 18 unit marking consisted

121▲   122▼

of forward fuselages (and usually wing upper surfaces) painted in red, with rear fuselages and tail units in white, with a black raven symbolizing Raben's name (Rabe – raven) carried immediately aft of the vertical colour division. Raben himself used a white raven for personal identification and marked this forward of the colour demarcation line, but this has yet to be applied to 479/17, seen

here with nine Albatros D Va's probably at Faches near Lille in late April 1918 (See Notes on Triplane Markings, Appendix IX).

122. Leutnant Krueger of Jasta 4 at Cappy in May 1918. His triplane has struts, fabric wheel covers and engine cowling painted in an off-white colour, the exact shade of which has not been determined. This was a recently adopted unit

marking since the black spiral fuselage band used by Jasta 4 previously on its Albatros D Va's and Pfalz D IIIa's had no application on the triplane. Note the high position of the circular magneto access aperture covered by an aluminium panel on the forward fuselage, the handiwork of Offizierstellvertreter Albrecht, the Jasta 4 Werkmeister.

▲123

123. The signal promoting Vizefeldwebel Edgar Scholz of Jasta 11 to commissioned rank arrived shortly after he was killed at Cappy on 2 May 1918 when he lost flying speed and stalled on take-off in 591/17 (Works No 2261) This view of his aircraft shows the cockpit interior, including the flexible drives running up to the guns and the location of engine controls. The simple air-slide with interconnected fuel needle of the bloctube carburettor was operated by Bowden cable from the left-hand side of the control column grip, but required an additional device to meter the fuel to cater for varying air density. The toothed quadrant and its lever, fitted with a long wooden handle, controlled this Benzinregler (fuel fine adjustment) and was placarded 'zu' (closed) in the aft position and 'auf' (open) when forward, and can be seen on the left upright steel tube fuselage member. If the Bowden cable failed, the throttle was spring-loaded to open; in such an emergency it could be closed by operating the rod with the T-handle, which can be seen on the right. The fuel cock on/off control is the rod projecting aft from the Benzinregeler quadrant, and the circular object just below the crash padding is the standard Bosch engine magneto switch. The blip-switch thumb push-button, for temporary cutting of the engine ignition for slow engine speed control, was fitted to the top of the control column grip and can just be seen. This triplane used the later pull-triggers for the guns, visible in the centre of the control column grip. The only instruments permanently installed in the cockpit (rpm indicator, magnetic compass and an oil pulsator) were situated almost at floor level and cannot be seen in this view. An altimeter was also carried, suspended on three shock-absorber springs. Its position varied, it was removable and generally of large size (some instruments had dials of 15cm (6in) diameter). Most pilots preferred much smaller altimeters (if they could get them), which were worn on the wrist like a watch.

124. This vertical view of the armament installation in Leutnant Alfred Greven's Jasta 12 triplane was obtained by standing the machine on its nose. The fitting of the Oigee reflector gunsight has caused the removal of the normal crash-pad protection on the gun butts and an altimeter can be seen suspended by small coiled springs against the sight fitting. Note the cut-down windscreen between the guns, rear-view mirror and the muzzle of the signal pistol projecting through the coaming adjacent to the external rack for the signal cartridges. The guns are fitted with two safety catches each, the forward crank type at fire, the crank handle on the port side being shortened to clear the sight; the two slender safety-catch fingers on the right-hand side at the rear of the butts are in the raised (safe) position.

124▶

125. Oberleutnant Karl Bolle, Staffelfuehrer of Jasta Boelcke, with his triplane, 413/17 (Works No 1997), in May 1918 on Halluin-Ost aerodrome. The ratio of its fuselage cross bars has been increased to improve recognition. The fuselage cross still has 5cm-wide white borders, although the 17 March official instruction called for these to be 15cm wide. The fuselage cross on the early Fokker D VII in the background has been applied correctly, but note how this has

reduced the size of the black cross, which at greater distances would cause this display to lose its cross definition. The fuselage bands carried by Bolle for identification are in the colours of his old regiment, Kuerassier-Regiment von Seydlitz Nr 7, a broad yellow band flanked by narrower bands of black and white. Bolle, who is wearing a captured RFC issue pull-on leather flying helmet, was one of several pilots who reverted to the use of a lap-strap in place of

the shoulder-strap safety harness fitted to the triplane; the end of the broad lap-strap can be seen at the edge of the cockpit. Note also the use of an Oigee telescopic sight and the barrel of the signal pistol protruding through the fuselage fabric immediately aft of the external stowage for the signal cartridges.

126. This Jasta Boelcke line-up at Halluin-Ost, probably in May, shows that the over-thick national insignia on rudders

and fuselages previously seen on this unit's triplanes has been altered, the width to length of the cross arms now being closer to the 1:4 ratio called for in the Kogenluft directive. Next to Kempf's distinctive triplane (probably 493/17) can be seen Baeumer's 204/17, with all wingtips painted black and still retaining its tailplane cross, now changed to Balkenkreuz form.

Boelcke, the unit in which Richthofen had served until he was given the command of Jagdstaffel 11 on 14 January 1917, and caused him to develop a more obvious red as his own colour, which he also felt was particularly appropriate for him personally, since red was the regimental colour of his old regiment, Uhlanen-Regiment Kaiser Alexander III Nr 1.

Such was Richthofen's success in aerial fighting in the next few months that his red Albatros D III became well known on both sides of the lines, and there was genuine concern among his pilots that the enemy might lay a trap for the 'Rote Kampfflieger' and made repeated requests to him to let them share the red colour. Eventually he relented and allowed red to be adopted as the unit identification marking in Jagdstaffel 11 from May 1917. In addition to the now uniform red fuselages that proclaimed all the aircraft as belonging to Jagdstaffel 11, each pilot carried a prominent marking in another colour for individual recognition – Richthofen's aeroplane being the only machine that used red also for this purpose. As described, Richthofen continued to use red to advantage as a leader's marking in Jagdgeschwader I, and after his death on 21 April 1918, 'Richthofen-red' remained a hallmark of aerial fighting prowess until the end of the war. The tales of its use are legion, but the reason for its choice was simple – ease of recognition.

NATIONAL INSIGNIA

DURING the nine months of Fokker V 5 triplane production, the national insignia applied to these aeroplanes at the factory was unique in that, even at the beginning of the period, it was already some twelve months out of date. This causes one immediately to question the efficiency of the personnel of Bauaufsicht 13, the Idflieg ZAK office at Schwerin taxed with monitoring manufacturing standards and supervising the final acceptance of aircraft.

The form of the iron cross used adhered to standards that had been introduced at the end of 1915. These were included in detail in the 1916 edition of Bau und Lieferungsvorschriften fuer Militaerflugzeuge (Construction and Delivery Requirements for Military Aeroplanes – BLV) which, when updated with a May 1917 amendment, of either manuscript changes or printed paper strips glued over the appropriate narrative sections, converted the 1916 BLV into the 1917 edition, and this was the current relevant document during the main period of triplane production.

The 1916 BLV specified that the black crosses were to be in the largest possible size and that the curved arms of the crosses should have a radius of 1.3 times the height, and the base of the cross arms should be 0.4 times the height. The crosses so formed were to be displayed above the top wings, below the lower wings and on each side of the fuselage on square white backgrounds, which were to be used on dark fabric or against dark colours to improve cross legibility. The rudder, which was painted white for the same reason, had to carry the cross in the centre of its area. The top wing and fuselage displays necessitated the white-painted backgrounds since the colour of these components was the streaked greenish/brown Fokker camouflage. On the wing undersurfaces, because of the sky camouflage light blue colour, white-painted backgrounds to the crosses were not really necessary, but the majority of triplanes used them. There were, however, some instances where the undersurface black crosses were applied directly onto the natural doped fabric, and since this was quite in keeping with the Idflieg instructions, one wonders why Fokker, in the interests of economy, did not use this system over the entire triplane production run.

What made this national insignia display out of date was that it did not reflect an Idflieg instruction dated 29 October 1916 to all aircraft manufacturers (Abt A Nr 310301). This introduced the requirement that crosses applied to dark coloured surfaces should only have a 5cm-wide white border (instead of the large white-painted backgrounds previously used). This stipulation was, of course, incorporated in the May 1917 BLV amendment, which stated '. . . when using dark and coloured fabrics or dark and coloured fuselages the 5cm-wide border is to be painted white'. Thus it appears that both Fokker and BA 13 had not amended their requirements documents and were using the out-of-date 1916 BLV.

When triplanes arrived at their allocated Jagdstaffeln, many of these units corrected the out-of-date national insignia by painting out the residue of the white backgrounds, leaving the regulation 5cm-wide white borders around the crosses. On occasion this was even done on the rudder, although this component had been considered a 'white' item since early 1915 in order that the cross carried upon it stood out clearly. It was not, however, sufficiently emphasized in the amended

127. Early in May JG I at Cappy gave up a number of its triplanes; initially three were assigned to Jasta 34b based at Foucaucourt where Leutnant Rudolf Stark flew 146/17. He was photographed standing beside this machine on 14 May after his first flight in the triplane. It is still in its Jasta 11 colours, and the rudder and fuselage crosses have been altered to have narrower-chord cross bars. The wing crosses have not been further changed. Later in May 146/17 was flown by Oberleutnant Greim, the Jasta 34b Staffelfuehrer, and in June the aircraft apparently passed to Leutnant Delling.

▲127

128. In May 1918 official Kogenluft photographers took a series of photographs of the component Jagdstaffeln of JG III based on Halluin-Ost aerodrome. In this scene nine triplanes of Jasta 26 are shown, their horizontal tail surfaces and rear fuselages banded in black and white as a unit marking. Most aircraft display the individual pilot's marking on the white fuselage band at, or immediately aft of, the cockpit, and this marking was also invariably carried on the centre of the top wing. (But note that the nearest triplane, its fuselage marked with two coloured bands, shows a '5' on the top wing.) The mechanics are about to help the pilots don their flying clothing, some of which can be seen on the ground on the right.

▲128   ▼129

129. Taxi-ing yellow-nosed triplane of Jasta 27 at Halluin-Ost aerodrome in May 1918. This machine was marked with a swastika-form cross on the fuselage for pilot identification, but part of the swastika has been obliterated in service. The wingtip mechanics are accompanied by two other ground personnel who obviously wanted to be included in the picture, posed for the official Kogenluft photographer.

instructions that the rudder should remain white and not merely have the 5cm-wide white border to its cross. As a result the remaining surface was often over-painted, sometimes in a particular Jagdstaffel unit marking colour (e.g., black in Jasta 12) or included in an individual pilot's marking (e.g., Manfred von Richthofen's red). Some units flew their triplanes as delivered with the out-of-date national insignia displays and were obviously not concerned that the large areas of white detracted from the effectiveness of their aeroplanes' uppersurface camouflage schemes, since the nature of their own unit and personal markings had long since disregarded this aspect.

A major change took place with the receipt of an order dated 17 March 1918, which was to be effected by 15 April, and called for the iron cross type national markings to be replaced by Balkenkreuze (straight-sided crosses). These were to have a 15cm-wide white border on wings and fuselage. The rudder was specifically mentioned in that it was to be painted white and carry the straight-sided black cross, and this effectively caused the malpractice in marking this component to cease.

It appears that there were, in fact, different versions of this order which originated from Kogenluft; and its interpretation by Idflieg, sent to the various BA offices of ZAK as 4077/18, does not appear to specify any particular ratio for the width to length of cross bars, but contained a sketch on a separate piece of paper showing how the new cross should appear. The Kogenluft document (41390 Fl III 17/3/18) contained a scale drawing showing the required ratio of 1:4 of cross bar width to length.

Acting on the Idflieg narrative instructions – especially if these were sent in telegraphic form and did not include the example sketch – meant that the initial instructions on the form of cross change reaching units at the front did not clearly show the requirements, since the first Balkenkreuze seen on the Fokker Dr I used, almost without exception, the widest part of the iron cross as a Balken or bar width, which was the easiest way to effect the change. Also, the white borders of most early altered fuselage crosses appear to have been of the previous 5cm size, due no doubt to attempts to mark the new crosses within the confines of the previous cross areas. The resulting insignia were difficult to define as crosses at a distance, the ratios of the cross bars being, at best, 1:3; and they were generally rapidly altered, either on receipt of more detailed instructions, or by a more thorough reading and appreciation of the order. The complainants were the pilots themselves, who had difficulty in identifying the thick crosses as German national insignia.

Wing crosses do not appear to have been further modified, since due to their greater size the manner of altering them to Balkenkreuze with a white border approximating to 15cm was generally satisfactory. Furthermore, access to the top wing was difficult and some triplanes even saw out their useful lives in mid-1918 with the factory-applied iron cross insignia at this location, complete with the original square white backgrounds. The rudder and fuselage crosses were generally altered until the required ratio of width to length of the cross bars was achieved. This was easy on the rudder, but the impossibility of applying a 15cm-wide white border on the fuselage without seriously reducing the size of the black cross meant that a large variety of crosses at this position were to be seen, few of them reflecting the exact nature of the 17 March Kogenluft instruction.

The markings of triplanes flown by Richthofen provide good examples of the changes that took place in the display of national insignia in the field over a period of only some three weeks. The rudder clause already mentioned caused his then current machine (425/17) to receive a white rudder instead of the red one previously marked on this aircraft, when the iron crosses were changed to Balkenkreuze, and this explains why, when he was brought down on 21 April 1918 in this machine, it was not entirely red in colour – i.e., it had a white rudder.

The form of the national insignia cross was to undergo two further changes. On 13 May 1918 an amendment (Kogenluft 43132 Fl III) to the 17 March Kogenluft order called for the vertical arms of the wing crosses to extend from leading to trailing edges – i.e., the cross had to occupy the full chord. In addition to the lengths of the vertical/horizontal cross arms having the unusual ratio of 5:4, the white outlines of the black crosses were discontinued at the ends of the cross bars, leaving only the white borders along the lengths of the cross bars. Furthermore, the ratio of cross bar width to length was given as 1:8 and the width of the white borders had to be one-quarter the width of the black cross bars. This instruction related only to wing national insignia, and crosses on fuselage and rudder were not mentioned; thus no further change was intended at these positions. However, some units at the front applied the new proportions to rudder and fuselage crosses, which resulted in some unusual decoration, especially on the rudder. Other units obviously hesitated before actioning this national insignia change which was a confusing amendment to what was already an untidy subject.

A new order was issued on 4 June 1918 (Kogenluft No 43650 Fl III) and although the only material change in

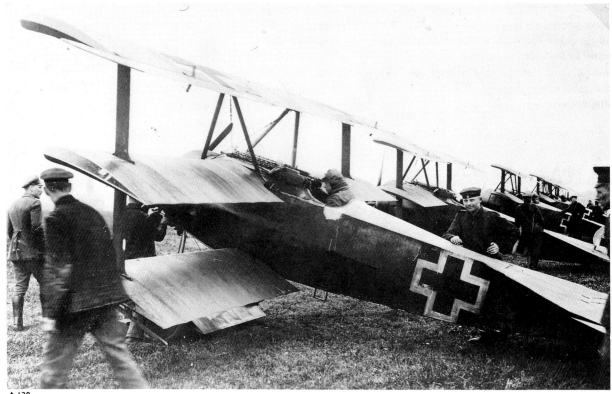

▲130

130. Official Kogenluft photograph of a line-up of Jasta 27 triplanes at Halluin-Ost in May 1918. A yellow nose, rear

▼131

fuselage, tailplane, elevators and all struts in this colour comprised the unit marking, individual pilot identification

markings usually being carried on the fuselage sides. Leutnant Rudolf Klimke is in the aircraft nearest the camera which,

according to numbers on the fuselage and centre-section struts, is 577/17 (Works No 2247). The guns have the late-type safety catches and can be seen at the butts in the down (armed) position. Klimke, who was of short stature, used a lap-strap for restraint instead of the usual shoulder-strap harness, since this allowed him easier access to the guns and did not restrict movements necessary to keep a good look-out behind.

131. Klimke with 577/17 showing his black anchor insignia on the yellow tailplane. He used this marking, which was also painted on the fuselage sides aft of the cockpit in yellow, at his mother's insistence, since she maintained that it symbolized 'Gute Hoffnung' (good hope) and when carried on her son's aeroplanes, no harm would befall him. It was partially successful. Although badly wounded on 21 September 1918, he survived the war and was credited with 16 victories.

this directive related to making the ratio of the vertical/horizontal cross arms 1:1, previous instructions on the subject were cancelled. It was obviously felt that some formations would only have part of the instructions already issued on the subject since 17 March, and the most efficient way to correct this anomaly was to start again. The instructions now issued had to be incorporated by 25 June 1918, and no further official changes relating to the display of national insignia were issued. Standardization had certainly not been achieved, and even on the decreasing numbers of Fokker triplanes used until the Armistice, there was considerable variety in the manner in which they displayed their national insignia.

ARMAMENT

TWIN LMG 08/15 machine-guns were installed immediately in front of the pilot, allowing him easy access to the bolt levers and the ammunition belts. Each gun was mounted on two tubular forked pillars, the rearmost of which provided adjustment in traverse and elevation. The forward top fuselage fairing was strengthened locally under each gun muzzle to reduce blast damage, by the provision of a square ribbed panel on either side of the streamlined fairing of the fuel contents gauge. These panels were riveted in place and were often left unpainted for easier crack detection.

The guns were synchronized by the Fokker Zentralsteuerung, enabling them to fire through the rotating propeller. When Fokker caused the standard 7.92mm-calibre infantry 08/15 machine-gun to be modified for aerial use in mid-1916, apart from replacing the heavy water-cooled jacket with a lighter perforated mantle for air-cooling, the original trigger and its associated safety catch were abandoned. The gun was fired by the engine when the firing lever on the control column was pressed. A Bowden cable engaging a dog-clutch allowed a rotating part of the engine to operate a flexible drive that gave the necessary firing impulses.

The gun was loaded by using the bolt crank on the right-hand side of the breech. Forward of this a safety catch was eventually provided whereby, when in its aft position, a crank, pivoted on a small bracket bolted to the side of the breech, blocked the bolt action. Before take-off the safety catch was moved forward and the bolt crank pushed forward, causing the lips of the bolt to grip a cartridge in the belt; backwards motion pulled the cartridge from the belt and moved it down the face of the bolt. The next forward movement inserted the round into the firing chamber and at the same time the next cartridge in the belt was gripped by the lips of the bolt as previously. The gun was now loaded and ready to fire. Firing the round caused the whole bolt to move aft under recoil, extracting the next round from the belt, moving the spent cartridge to the bottom of the bolt and placing the previously selected round in line with the firing chamber. Forward motion was via the recoil spring; this ejected the spent cartridge, gripped the next round in the belt and fired the round in the firing chamber. This sequence continued as long as the engine was allowed to supply the firing impulses.

The basic ammunition for the 08/15 machine-gun was called *S*-Munition (Spitzgeschoss – ordinary pointed bullet or ball ammunition) which had an initial velocity of approx. 900 metres per second, and its accuracy, especially at short ranges, was extremely high. However, the need to provide ammunition capable of penetrating armour-plate brought about the *P*-Munition (Panzer), also known as *SmK*-Munition (*S*pitzgeschoss *m*it Stahl*k*ern). This had a centre core of the finest tungsten steel, which was pressed into the hollow bullet with a lead lining. The manufacture of this round was not easy, but the results were excellent and it could penetrate the best armoured steel of 11mm thickness at a range of 100 metres.

The need for bullets to leave a trace, which the gunner used to correct his aim, led to the *L*-spur-Munition (Lichtspurgeschoss) (officially *SmK-L* 'spur – *S*pitzgeschoss *m*it Stahl*k*ern und *L*euchtsatz). The Germans, instead of using the whole bullet to carry the tracer composition, which included an ingredient to delay its burning to give traces over extended ranges, retained approx. 50 per cent of the steel core, thus preserving the hit-effectiveness of the round. The trace was a small flame which emerged from a hole at the base of the bullet and was visible at distances up to 1,000 metres.

The desire to make the destruction of observation balloons more certain led to the development of the phosphorus bullet. Based on ammunition used by the British, it was initially known as Phosphor-F but was designated Ph-Munition from March 1917 (officially *S*. Pr.-Munition – *S*pitzgeschoss mit *p*hosphorfuelling).

132. Oberleutnant Hermann Goering, Staffelfuehrer of Jagdstaffel 27, in his triplane which, although its number cannot be read, is almost certainly 206/17 (Works No 1925), an aircraft of the unit that was still on strength in July 1918. Goering, who used areas of white on his triplane for personal identification, had all struts, tail unit, rear fuselage, engine cowling and wheel covers in this colour. Empty cartridge cases were ejected overboard from below the guns and were a distraction for some pilots, including Goering who had all his aircraft fitted with simple baffles made from sheet metal to deflect the spent cases away from his immediate vicinity; that for the right-hand gun can be seen on the coaming ahead of the cockpit, immediately aft of the guide for the ammunition belt. Signal pyrotechnics were carried externally to lessen the risk of setting fire to the aircraft. Note that Goering is using a small ring backsight on his right-hand gun, instead of the standard 'vee' type with which his left-hand gun is fitted.

133. This was the triplane seen fourth from right in the Jasta 6

▲132

line-up at Léchelle and is here depicted at Cappy on the strength of Jasta 5 in May with Balkenkreuze national insignia. Some of the previous markings have been over-painted, obliterating the Jasta 6 black and white stripes on tailplane and elevators and Beckmann's red fuselage band with its

superimposed white wavy line, but the original lightning flash marking on the fuselage side is still legible. The aircraft's serial number is in doubt, since works numbers seen on interplane struts and rudder appear to come from different aircraft. It is known that 556/17 was allocated to Jasta 5 and, apart

from the visible markings mentioned, confirmation that this was a Jasta 6 machine is provided by the size and location of the rectangular magneto access panel on the forward fuselage, which was the standard pattern adopted by the Werkmeister of Jasta 6 for all his triplanes.

▼133

The hollow bullet was filled with yellow phosphorus and sealed at the base with a plug. A small hole in the side of the bullet, sealed with a very low melting-point solder, allowed the expanding phosphorus, warmed by firing, to issue, and it was its contact with the air that caused it to burn. Improved Ph-Munition possessed an increased and more reliable effect. This was achieved by having a loose lead plug at the base of the phosphorus charge which, on hitting the target, accelerated forward and forced the phosphorus out, or even caused the shell of the bullet to burst. An additional advantage of this ammunition was that the phosphorus streaming out of the round gave a good tracer trail.

The greatest difficulty in the manufacture of all these rounds designed for specific purposes lay in the fact that they should all, ideally, possess the same ballistic properties. This, however, was not possible due to their differing weights. Since the trajectories were similar at the shorter ranges, they were used together in the same belt and the visual indication of Ph-Munition was used for the correct placing of the burst of fire at ranges up to 400 metres and that of SmK-L'spur for ranges beyond this. In air fighting where shorter ranges were used (those of less than 50 metres were not uncommon), no undue difficulties were experienced, except that the spread of the bullets was naturally greater at the longer ranges.

As explained, the operation of the gun depended on recoil, and the tension of the recoil spring could easily be set to cater for the type of ammunition in the belt. However, when using mixed rounds, cartridges had different recoil values and this was the most frequent cause of the gun jamming. Various muzzle-boosters were used to cater for the different types of ammunition, but the most reliable operation was obtained when one gun was armed with one type of ammunition and its associated recoil spring adjusted accordingly: for example, one belt could be loaded with Ph-Munition, and the other with SmK and SmK-L'spur in the ratio of 4 to 1. This practice was generally maintained, but it is known that sometimes both guns carried a high percentage of Ph-Munition, the use of which should have been supported by a written authorization stating the pilot was engaged in attacking hostile balloons, in order to secure his protection if he became a PoW. However, this rule, based on the 'pain of death' Article of the 1908 Hague International Convention, had fallen into disuse by 1918; although, curiously, some Jagdstaffeln still religiously applied it despite the fact that Germany was not a signatory of the convention.

The synchronizing gear was driven off the large gear wheel at the rear of the engine that was used to drive the magneto and oil pump engine auxiliaries. A spur gear meshed with the large gear wheel and had three output drives: two via Bowden cable-operated dog-clutches for the flexible drives for the guns, and the flexible drive to the rpm indicator. Because these drives came from the lower part of the engine's main bearer plate and could not be routed directly upwards and aft because of the fuel/oil tank and the ammunition boxes, they were led underneath these items. This necessitated flexible drives of considerable length for the guns that changed direction through 90° as they were led upwards immediately aft of the loaded ammunition box to connect to the bottom of the gun breeches. No trouble appears to have arisen because of this extended routeing. The drive to the rpm indicator was shorter and more direct and this meant that the instrument was situated at a low level in the cockpit, but was easy to read since its dial was angled slightly upwards.

The trigger bar actuator on the gun end of the flexible drive was at first a cam with two lobes, but this was later replaced by an ingenious device whereby a cruciform impeller caused four steel balls, thrown out by centrifugal force, to work the trigger. The four impulses per revolution of the drive increased the rate of fire, and was less subject to wear, since the balls could be easily replaced. The two dog-clutches on the flexible drives for the guns were operated by Bowden cable from two thumb push-levers on the control column; thus the guns could be fired independently. Also fitted was a pull trigger which fell naturally under the forefinger of the right hand and operated both guns simultaneously. This latter device was a Richthofen idea, made by Fokker and already used in JG I on other aircraft types. It was a standard fitment on early Fokker Dr Is but late-production triplanes used a modified version which dispensed with the thumb pushes entirely, replacing them with two pull triggers, conveniently located in the centre of the control column grip and worked by the first two fingers of the right hand, allowing the guns to be fired either independently or simultaneously.

Cartridges were contained in a hemp belt, and although the capacity of the ammunition box allowed 650 rounds for each gun to be carried, normally 500 rounds per gun were used to save weight; both loaded belts were carried in the same ammunition box. Empty cartridge cases were ejected overboard from the bottom of the guns, while the empty belts were collected in a special box situated immediately in front of the box for the loaded belts, via curved aluminium tubes which had spring-loaded access flaps near the feed blocks. Despite careful checking of rounds and loading of belts – an activity in which all conscientious pilots engaged with

134. Six triplanes and an Albatros D Va of Jasta 14 on Phalempin aerodrome in the VI Armee area on 23 May, whence the unit had moved from Masny on 11 April in readiness for the attack on Kemmel Hill. Leutnant Werner's replacement aircraft on the right is apparently 583/17 (Works No 2253); its fuselage bands have yet to be painted on the decking aft of the cockpit. National insignia changes are taking place and Heinecke parachute packs can be seen on the fuselage deckings of the nearest triplanes.

▲134 ▼135

135. Vizefeldwebel Johann Puetz of Jasta 34b wearing a captured British Sidcot suit, a garment coveted by the German pilots because of its lighter weight compared with their own issue 'Fliegerkombination', and because its pockets could be used while sitting in the cockpit. This triplane is fitted with a small-area aileron on the starboard side. Although its serial number is not known, the machine originated from JG I, and was almost certainly from the batch of triplanes delivered with asymmetrical ailerons in late December 1917. Despite the date of the photograph being May 1918, the under-wing national insignia is still of the iron cross type; crosses at the other locations on the airframe had been changed to Balkenkreuze. The machine is marked with a green engine cowling and two green fuselage bands aft of the cockpit, these being Puetz's personal identification markings. The rear fuselage and tail unit were over-painted whitish-silver, denoting Jasta 34b. The propeller is probably a Lorenzen 'Pertrax', which was of similar shape to that made by Heine. Both Heine Propellerwerk and Lorenzen Luftschraubenbau did not apply their company trademark symbols as transfers to their products, as Axial did, but embossed their names into the wood.

136. Leutnant Werner's triplane crashed in the British lines, 9 June 1918. A detailed comparison of the manner of camouflage streaking and repair patches show that this is the same aircraft shown in the Jasta 14 line-up photograph. Reportedly being flown by Gefreiter Preiss, a junior pilot of the unit, the painting of the fuselage bands has been completed, but the original Schwerin-applied top wing national insignia has not been modified. A British report on this aeroplane stated that all wings were dated 22 March and that Fl No 1285 ('Fl' means Flaeche – wing) was marked on the machine. The report also gave the Works number as 2253, which equates with 583/17 in the Fokker production listing. The colours of the fuselage bands were given as red and white, thus Preiss apparently adopted red to over-paint and complete the already partly applied fuselage bands when he was allocated this machine. (Werner himself was by now flying one of the new Fokker D VII biplanes, a number of which had been delivered to Jasta 14.) The original British basic report on the crashed triplane stated that its number was 588/17. The location of the fuselage bands meant that the military designation and number would be obliterated in part; thus the number quoted was obviously a deduction. (That it was incorrect, we have seen, since 588/17 was the number of Wenzl's machine.) The aircraft should also have carried its military number, stamped on several metal plates fixed to the structure in accordance with the BLV requirements. Their location on the Fokker Dr I are unknown, but were probably on the root-end ribs of the wings and would only be visible when the aircraft was dismantled. The type was no longer new, and from the contents of the reports seen this does not appear to have been done during its examination after capture. If such a number plate was visible externally, it may have been 'souvenired' before the arrival of RAF Intelligence.

137. Oberleutnant Robert Greim, Staffelfuehrer of Jasta 34b and Gruja of Jagdgruppe 'Greim', with his silver-tailed 521/17 (Works No 2189) on Foucaucourt aerodrome, June 1918. Greim's personal markings comprised a red engine cowling and the two red fuselage bands shown. He flew this aircraft during the month mentioned, alternating with his Albatros D Va and Fokker D VII, but on 27 June during a combat with a Bristol Fighter, his triplane's engine cowling flew off and damaged the top wing leading-edge and broke the port bottom interplane strut. Greim was able to land safely, but there is no indication that he flew 521/17 again. On 16 July 1918 the triplane was destroyed during a British air attack on Foucaucourt.

136▲ 137▼

138. When Jasta 6 and 11 of Jagdgeschwader I were re-equipped with Fokker D VIIs in May 1918, some of their better triplanes found their way to Jasta 4. This is Leutnant Hans Kirschstein's old machine, 586/17 (Works No 2256), which is depicted on the front cover of this book. Later it was flown, still in its original markings, by Leutnant Ernst Udet, Jasta 4's Staffelfuehrer, who added his personal 'LO' insignia to the fuselage sides. This is probably the last photograph taken of this machine after a forced landing in June, following an engine failure when, apparently, a detached cylinder removed the cowling in flight and tore the metal engine bulkhead. Note the holes in the lower surface of the upper wing caused by flying debris. The Jasta 6-pattern magneto access panel is apparent.

▲138

▲139   ▼140

139. Ernst Udet sitting in what was evidently his last triplane, 593/17 (Works No 2263), on Beugneux – Cramoiselle aerodrome in mid-June. The small presentation of his 'LO!' insignia is a chalk drawing on the fabric to show the painter the desired layout, part of the full-size outline of which can just be discerned at the bottom right on the original photograph. This triplane also carried a large white chevron on its tailplane and elevators and was apparently a new machine that did not have any additional access panels on its forward fuselage (see Appendix IX).

140. Reportedly 558/17 (Works No 2228) was crashed by Vizefeldwebel Fritz Rumey of Jasta 5. If the serial number is correct, Leutnant von Hippel flew this machine for the first time on 3 June and that was his final flight before leaving Jasta 5. The oil pump access panel confirms that this triplane was originally on the strength of Jasta 6; that unit's black and white tailplane and elevator stripes have been over-painted, but whether this was in the green colour used by Jasta 5 as a unit identification marking is not known.

the weapons mechanics – guns jammed for a variety of reasons. The most serious was due to Hulsenreiser (broken cartridge case) and this could not be cleared in the air. Faulty feeds could be cleared by operating the bolt lever and pulling on the empty belt via the small spring-loaded access flaps. This needed both hands and since the Fokker Dr I did not have any device for locking the control column or any longitudinal trim other than throttle setting, pilots had to hold the control column between their knees when performing this act.

Gunsights were the normal circular cross-wire fore-sight and simple 'vee' backsight. Sometimes the cross-wires were cut away so that the target remained unobstructed, and, depending on what eye the pilot used for aiming, the appropriate 'vee' backsight was replaced on occasion by a small ring-type backsight. Various tubular sights were also used, notably that made by the Oigee optical company of Berlin-Schoeneberg. Although externally resembling the British Aldis sight, the Oigee tubular sight differed from the Aldis in that it was a true telescopic sight with a ×3 magnification. In early 1918 Oigee received a contract for an unspecified number of reflector sights, and the first six of these 'electrical aiming devices' were sent to the front for operational trials in March, one of them being fitted to the Fokker Dr I flown by Leutnant Greven of Jagdstaffel 12 in May. In this sight, the brightness of an electric bulb in the base of the instrument, illuminated by a 6-volt battery, was controlled by a variable resistance. Light was projected upwards through a matt glass screen onto the surface of a transparent ground-glass mirror set at an angle of 45°. The pilot saw this illumination as a small red disc, which appeared to float free in the mirror, and was perfectly visible even in bright sunlight. Aiming was exceptionally easy since this did not depend on an aiming line, and the pilot simply steered the disc of light onto the target. This system gave better results than those obtained with the Oigee tubular telescopic sight because the field of vision was not reduced during aiming.

Richthofen considered that the most important items on a fighter aircraft were the machine-guns, saying that '. . . a good working gun is better than a good running engine'. He also stated that a fighter pilot had to be so completely au fait with his guns that when he experienced trouble with them, the reason for the malfunction should be immediately obvious to him. Richthofen made his pilots responsible for the performance of their guns: if the pilot did his work well enough, jammed guns did not happen; if they did, it was the pilot and not the Waffenmeister or the armament mechanics that got the full blast of Richthofen's wrath. He was uncompromising about the care needed in making up ammunition belts and required that cartridges be checked with an accuracy gauge before loading them into the belts with the special belt-loading tool (Gurtfueller 16) which ensured that each individual cartridge was inserted into the belt-pockets with the same tension. This was time-consuming, but the time to do it properly had to be found, which was easy if bad weather prevented or curtailed flying, but in good weather when flying activity was high, this job had to be done at night. The guns were adjusted at the butts until at a range of 150 metres two parallel lines of hits were produced. Air-firing was a feature of continuation training that Richthofen insisted upon. Pilots were required to participate in this, shooting at a ground target to verify both the accurate sighting of their guns and the pilot's ability to use the weapons effectively.

The LMG 08/15 was, despite the modifications mentioned, still basically the same internally as the infantry weapon, its rate of fire being approximately 600 rounds per minute. Late in 1917 there were several meetings between the Waffen-und-Munitions Beschaffungs Amt (Munitions Department of the War Ministry – Wumba) and Idflieg to discuss measures necessary to improve the gun's aerial application and to investigate the recent repeated complaints about the poor quality of the working parts of the gun (which Wumba stated to be due to insufficiently hardened components). One result was the formation of a specialist aviation weapons detachment which was located at the Koenigliche Gewehrfabrik, Spandau, where the guns were manufactured. This accelerated the programme of improvement to make the LMG 08/15, whose triggering had been designed for hand use, more compatible with the synchronization drives used to fire it. The internal mechanism was modified and lightening the firing pin system increased the rate of fire by 50 rounds per minute. Changes were also made to the stops of the bolt lever, and over the next few months guns appeared with improved safety catches, round-counters and more efficient loading levers. However, it seems that few of these modifications were installed in the Fokker Dr I, the bulk of this machine's production having been achieved before these improved weapons became generally available.

▲ 141

▼ 142

141. Leutnant Hans Pippart, Staffelfuehrer of Jasta 19, being helped with his 'Flieger-kombination'. His triplane is 471/17 (Works No 2097) and shows that in addition to the normal gunsights, central sights are fitted, the foresight being attached to a raised column, riveted to the top of the engine cowling. Most fighter pilots dispensed with the Morell anemometer-type airspeed indicator, seen attached to the starboard upper interplane strut. However, despite the apparent simplicity of this instrument, it was an extremely efficient means of providing airspeed readings, and was less subject to density and temperature errors at altitude than a comparable pitot-static airspeed indicator. The lack of streakiness on wings and fuselage indicate that Pippart's machine has been over-painted; his personal disc marking, seen on the fuselage side and decking, was also repeated in the centre of the upper mainplane.

142. The fame that surrounded the use of the Fokker Dr I by the elite Jagdgeschwadern meant that when these machines were replaced by the new Fokker D VII, many pilots in other units were able to try the triplane, and it was not unusual to find at least one example on the strength of some Jagdstaffeln during the summer of 1918. One such was the triplane used by Leutnant Gerhard Anders, Staffelfuehrer of Jasta 73, seen flying, apparently in June 1918, from St Rémy le Petit aerodrome.

MAINTENANCE

THE most technically knowledgeable man in the Jagdstaffel was the Werkmeister, a senior NCO who was the product of a special training course at Doeberitz, entry to which was limited to technical personnel who had already a number of years' experience. His task in the Jagdstaffel was to address the day-to-day problems that arose in keeping the aircraft serviceable. In the Jagdstaffeln some pilots were allocated additional responsibilities to flying, and that of the Technical Officer was a typical example. Although the Werkmeister was subordinate to the TO, the latter did not necessarily possess any special qualifications or experience related to the position that he held. He was essentially a fighter pilot, and took advice from the Werkmeister on technical matters, being concerned mainly with the correctness of the associated documentation.

The aeroplanes 'belonged' to the Werkmeister, who usually lavished something approaching paternal care on them. The possessiveness that grew from this association meant that he 'allowed' the mechanics to work on the aircraft, and also 'tolerated' the pilots flying his charges. If a pilot mishandled a machine and damaged it, he (regardless of rank) was normally more concerned about what the Werkmeister would say than any reprimand from the Staffelfuehrer.

The Werkmeister in Jagdstaffel 36 appears to have been one of the first of these senior NCOs responsible for leaving permanent signs of his handiwork on the triplanes under his care. In Jasta 36 it is apparent that the triplanes were, from receipt, modified in at least two ways to facilitate maintenance work on them, and the features that resulted serve as a means of identifying the triplanes in this unit.

The only access to the area behind the engine provided by Fokker was a large panel on the bottom of the forward fuselage, hinged at its forward edge and retained by spring-loaded fasteners. Mechanics had to crawl under the triplane and crouch or stand up in the opening provided in order to work on the engine auxiliaries and the dog-clutches of the machine-gun synchronization gear. Adjustment of the latter was reasonably easy since these clutches and drives were located on the lower half of the engine's main bearer plate, or thrust box, and accessibility to the bloctube carburettor was also provided for; but magneto and oil pump maintenance from below were awkward operations. Although the components themselves were fitted

on the engine centre-line either side of the induction pipe, the items that required frequent attention were the magneto HT lead to the distributor, with its spring-loaded carbon brush, and the air bleed cock or screwed plug on the upper part of the oil pump body.* The former was mounted on the upper half of the engine thrust box and access to it from above entailed disconnection of the centre-section bracing wires and removal of the guns to get the forward fuselage fairing off. In Jasta 36, holes were cut in the forward fuselage sides above the thrust line and were covered by circular aluminium panels to simplify access to the magneto on the left-hand side, and to the oil pump on the right-hand side. The ease with which the unit's mechanics could now perform on these engine auxiliaries must have made them eternally grateful to their forward-thinking Werkmeister.

The plywood-covered wing fairing of the undercarriage axle came in for a great deal of abuse, especially on rough aerodrome surfaces, and tended to work loose, and this could alter its angular setting. The aerofoil-shaped fairing was rigged at 2° positive incidence and its area of $1.18m^2$ provided a useful amount of lift and minimum drag, as long as this incidence setting was retained. If allowed to change, it adversely affected the aircraft's performance. The axle itself was housed in an aluminium spanwise box and was sprung by rubber bungee shock cord wrapped around two bobbins at each end, and the ribs of the axle wing fairing were attached to the axle housing box. If the wing fairing needed securing, there was no means of internal access without opening up the plywood and re-attaching it again after repair. In Jasta 36, auxiliary struts or rods of circular cross-section were made up, apparently by the unit's blacksmith, to a standard pattern since they were identical on all the Staffel's triplanes. These fittings were fixed to the rear undercarriage struts with bolted clips and attached to the undercarriage wing's trailing-edge, thus bracing it more positively in service. As stated, these auxiliary struts were fitted to Jasta 36 triplanes immediately after arrival and before the fairing had any

*The distributor ring which fed the magneto HT current to the sparking plugs was fixed to the thrust cover and rotated with the engine. It was subject to contamination by oil thrown by centrifugal force off the large gearwheel which drove the gears of the engine auxiliaries and required frequent cleaning. To prevent cavitation of the oil pump, the air bleed was opened until the flow of oil did not reveal any air bubbles and was then closed. This had to be done at regular intervals and always before the 'first flight of the day'.

▲143

143. The identities of the two non-commissioned pilots, who seem amused by the 'Marie' marking on the fuselage band of 489/17 (Works No 2115) of Jasta 14 on Phalempin aerodrome, are unknown. The upper wing national insignia, despite being of Balkenkreuze type, are still displayed on square white backgrounds, which seems to have been a feature of crosses in this unit. Note its use on the fuselages of the two machines in the background.

144. Unknown pilot of Jasta 14 with his three mechanics, whose triplane shows non-standard numbering at the base of the starboard lower interplane strut, indicating that this machine is 466/17 (Works No 2092). The national insignia displayed are based on the 13 May Kogenluft instruction, which applied to wings only, and called for the vertical/horizontal cross arms to have the unusual ratio of 5:4. Here (incorrectly) the fuselage and rudder crosses have been changed in sympathy. Less than a month later new instructions caused the deletion of this peculiar insignia. Probable date of this photograph is late May/early June 1918.

▼144

chance of working loose, and so preserved the intended lift and drag properties of this component.

One would have thought that such practical innovations introduced by one Werkmeister would have been automatically adopted by the others and their use spread throughout the Jagdgeschwader, but it seems that this was not so. To some extent the Jasta 36 undercarriage wing fairing bracing system was adopted by Jasta Boelcke, but this unit's bracings were not the same, nor were all Jasta Boelcke triplanes so fitted. Those that were, show that their undercarriage wing bracing struts were not exactly alike, which suggests that they were made up individually and used as required, apparently once the axle fairing showed signs of working loose. Other triplanes were to be seen with similar bracing struts, but the use of these was uncommon except within the two Jagdstaffeln mentioned.

The Werkmeister of Jasta 6 also took the precaution of modifying all triplanes on receipt by fitting standardized access panels on the forward fuselage sides. These were centrally situated on the thrust line, rectangular in shape and generally left unpainted. Triplanes in Jasta 11 were not all modified, and those that had access panels used a circular shape fitted on the thrust line. Werkmeister Albrecht of Jasta 4 adopted the location and type of access panel used by Jasta 36, and these appear to have been installed on receipt of new triplanes on 20 April. Later machines of this unit, whose access panels did not conform, were obviously second-hand aircraft from other units; examples seen can be identified as previously having been on the strengths of Jasta 6 and 11.

Such access panels on the fuselages of other units' triplanes appeared in a variety of shapes and at a number of locations. Generally there is little uniformity, suggesting that the almost haphazard method used to install them was occasioned, not by forward planning, but by the need to gain access to some defective component that required rectification.

The location and shape of the standardized access panels used on the triplanes of Jasta 4, 6 and 36 were akin to the signatures of the Werkmeister concerned, and when such aircraft were over-painted and used by new owners, these features generally allow the origin of the aeroplanes to be determined. However, the majority of triplanes never had access panels fitted, indicating that mechanics in most Jagdstaffeln had to manage as best they could, using the large bottom tray panel provided by Fokker.

Three mechanics were assigned to each triplane in the Jagdstaffel. The first mechanic held Unteroffizier (corporal) rank and was directly responsible to the Werkmeister for the serviceability of the aircraft. The Unteroffizier did all the really technical work on the machine, assisted by his second mechanic who was a Gefreiter (lance-corporal). Both these mechanics were fully trained, highly skilled men and were completely au fait with airframe and engine, in most cases having attended manufacturer's courses on their subjects. The third man, who liked to call himself a Monteur (mechanic), was actually unskilled and usually a Flieger (private). Apart from refuelling and cleaning the aircraft, he was essentially a helper for the two skilled mechanics. He collected the petrol from the fuel dump in standard issue 30-litre cylindrical metal drums with conical tops for pouring, and also ensured that a similar smaller container was fully charged with rotary-engine lubricating oil. These supplies were kept in the hangar tent beside the triplane, together with the mechanics' tool boxes. Special tools for major engine work and rigging instruments, such as incidence boards and spirit levels or clinometers, were kept under lock and key by the Werkmeister who signed them out as required to the respective Unteroffiziere. Machine-guns and ammunition were maintained and issued by a specialist weapons section, the Waffenmeisterei, which was also responsible for signal pistols and cartridges.

FLYING

MOST triplane pilots were introduced to rotary-engine handling by flying the Fokker D V. This aircraft was powered by a 100hp Oberursel U I, which worked on the Gnome principle and did not have an effective throttle. Engine speed was controlled by varying the amount of fuel allowed to reach the simple carburettor jet by means of a Benzin-regler (fuel fine adjustment). Once the optimum position for this lever had been found on its quadrant, the engine ran at full throttle, and was usually slowed by manipulation of the Schnirpsknopf (blip switch) on the control column. Depressing this button cut the ignition, but the flywheel effect of the spinning engine caused it to continue rotation; before the engine lost momentum and

145. There were many flying accidents with the triplane, and this one obviously hit the ground at a high rate of descent in a level attitude, collapsing the undercarriage and causing the fuselage to fail at the cockpit, before going over onto its back and telescoping the centre-section struts. This is a Jasta 14 aircraft despite its fuselage not bearing the horizontal black and white stripe unit marking. The pilot of 475/17 (Works No 2101) was probably Leutnant Emmerich Honig, who was killed when he stalled and crashed on 4 June 1918 on Phalempin aerodrome.

▲145

146. A seldom seen view of the triplane's under surfaces, showing the central lacing seam of the fuselage belly fabric bag. Due to the direction of propeller rotation, ejected engine oil and exhaust dirt from the bottom of the cowling were unevenly distributed by the slipstream, so the port wings received more of this contamination than the starboard ones. Rienau said that this was one of his many crashes on the Fokker Dr I, in this case in June 1918. It appears that a heavy landing bent the starboard wheel axle and kinked the rear undercarriage strut, causing the machine to turn upside-down.

▲146   ▼147

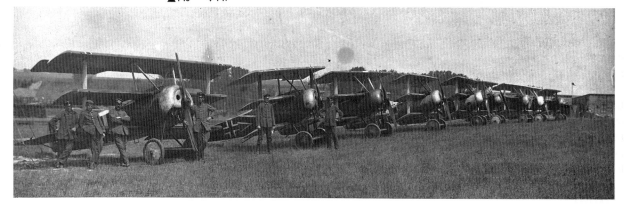

147. Engine problems due to poor-quality lubricating oil became more frequent with increasing summer temperatures and caused the triplanes of JG II to be relegated to less offensive work. This meant that by early June the operational effectiveness of Jasta 12, 13 and 19 was seriously reduced. Only Jasta 15 had Fokker D VIIs and as further machines of this type arrived, the recipients were Jasta 13 and 19. Only Jasta 12, despite a high unserviceability rate, soldiered on completely equipped with the triplane until 24 June when Kofl orders caused the machines to be given up to AFP XVIII. The heterogeneous collection of nine triplanes seen here are the last Jasta 12 machines lined up on Les Mesnil aerodrome shortly before being ferried to the AFP.

stopped, releasing the Schnirpsknopf caused the engine to pick up again, but before it could reach high rpm, the button was pressed once more to cut the ignition. This frequent application of the Schnirpsknopf (called schnirpsen or blipping) kept the power at a low level, but the hazard of fire was great, since the rotating engine continued to suck fuel into the crankcase and cylinders, and releasing the blip switch could result in back-fires through the air intake, which on the Fokker D V was inside the forward fuselage. If prolonged power-off flight was required – e.g., when gliding – some measure of engine speed control was available by closing the Benzinregler; but frequent use of the Schnirpsknopf was a sure sign of a Gnome-trained pilot.

On the Oberursel UR II fitted to the triplane, a throttle lever was provided, as well as a Benzinregler, thus less use of the Schnirpsknopf was intended. In fact, over-indulgence of schnirpsen on the UR II, which was modelled on the 110hp Le Rhône, could be harmful to the engine and should only have been used with the throttle fully closed. Due to their training, triplane pilots did not always do this and there seems little doubt that engine mishandling was responsible for some of the many engine failures on the triplane.

The throttle lever (on the left-hand side of the control column grip) worked the air-slide with its interconnected fuel needle of the bloctube carburettor, and controlled the engine power as long as the Benzinregler was in the correct position. Finding this position varied from day to day and depended on the atmospheric conditions. Normal practice after starting the engine was to open the throttle and adjust the Benzinregler to give maximum rpm (about 1,100 at the chocks) with smooth running. The position of the lever was noted since this was required as a take-off setting. The throttle was then closed and the Benzinregler setting adjusted accordingly. This gave approximately 800rpm, which was too fast for safe taxi-ing on smooth ground, and the engine was blipped as necessary until the aircraft was at the take-off position. The throttle was now opened for take-off, the previously found position of the Benzinregler lever having been set on the quadrant. The length of the take-off run was extremely short, and the triplane would leap off the ground after a run of only some 50 metres, even in still-air conditions, and climb initially at a rate of 2,000 feet per minute.

As the aircraft climbed, due to the decrease in air density, less fuel was required to maintain a correct fuel/air mixture and it was necessary to close the Benzinregler slightly to obtain this. The engine speed generally aimed for was 1,200rpm, but due to the reducing air density the engine power decreased with increase in altitude (despite the continual correction of the fuel/air mixture), until eventually the power was insufficient to enable the aircraft to continue climbing; this decided the triplane's ceiling, which was around 6,000 metres.

Pilots flew by feel and little use was made on the triplane of the strut-type anemometer airspeed indicator normally fitted to German aeroplanes. Because of the gyroscopic effect of the rotary engine – where the applied force to the gyroscope is resolved as a force at 90° in the direction of rotation – the nose went down in right-hand turns and up in left-hand turns. Thus in steep turns to maintain a constant altitude, left rudder was required in both cases. Although the terms have long since disappeared from textbooks on flying instruction, these were understandably referred to as top rudder and bottom rudder respectively.

Descent was carried out by closing the throttle and the Benzinregler completely. The engine then ceased firing but still rotated due to the windmilling propeller. Power was restored by opening the Benzinregler to the appropriate setting for the altitude. Landing approaches were made with the throttle closed and the Benzinregler at a setting that allowed the engine to keep firing, and use was made of the Schnirpsknopf to reduce power further. The pilot's view of the ground over the nose was not good but large cut-outs were provided in the trailing-edges of the centre wing roots to improve downward visibility, that on the left-hand side being commonly used. The triplane was always three-pointed, and was brought in fast enough to maintain effective aileron control, flattening out very low over the ground.

Because of its configuration the triplane's centre of gravity was higher than that of rotary-engined biplanes, and in the loaded state was 34.5cm aft of the leading-edge of the centre mainplane and above the thrust line. This made it laterally unstable on the ground and this was the reason why wingtip skids were fitted. If during the very short hold-off when landing, the aircraft was allowed to stall from a low height, the left wing always dropped first, setting up a lateral rocking motion which was accentuated by rough aerodrome surfaces. Wingtip landings were common, but the wingtip skids lessened the risk of such landings becoming ground loops or even cartwheels. After landing, the Schnirpsknopf was released to catch the engine before it stopped and the triplane blipped its way in to the tents where any close-in manoeuvring was done with the help of mechanics on the wingtips.

The triplane did not possess any inherent stability and as a result had to be flown all the time. It was this touchiness that made it such a wonderful dog-fighter. Its

148. Jagdstaffel 5 had received a full complement of ex-JG I triplanes early in May, but with the increasing availability of the new Fokker D VII biplane fighters, the triplanes were being gradually replaced. That the type was still in use by Jasta 5 on 22 July is shown by this photograph of the crashed machine of Leutnant Willi Schuster, who was killed at Cappy on a practice flight in one of the few remaining triplanes in the unit on that date.

▲148

149. No details of the capture of Raben's 479/17 are known, but it is obviously a matter of considerable interest to this group of French personnel. The crosses on the upper wing have been altered to full-chord and their proportions reflect the incorporation of instructions contained in the Kogenluft directive of 5 June 1918. Leutnant Raben and his Jasta 18 were by this time flying Fokker D VIIs, and although 479/17 has retained its original colour scheme, it was doubtless being operated by some other unit when it fell into French hands.

▲149 ▼150

150. Due to the shortage of aircraft generally, the gradually diminishing number of triplanes continued to serve with the front-line units until late in 1918. This is a Jasta 36 triplane, apparently in August since components of Fokker E V parasol monoplanes are included in the photograph. The upper wing national insignia conforming to the proportions in the last directive on the subject have finally forsaken the inboard position used on the triplane's upper wing and appear, as originally called for in the 17 March instruction, at the wingtips.

151▲   152▼

151. Leutnant Josef Jacobs, Staffelfuehrer of Jasta 7, with his Clerget-powered triplane on St Marguerite aerodrome, probably in late August. Jacobs, who survived the war, was credited with 41 victories, a high proportion of them obtained in his two black-painted triplanes, 450/17 (Works No 2075) and 470/17 (Works No 2096), which were both periodically powered by captured Clerget engines. The machine shown is probably 470/17 which was written off in a crash on 3 October. Even after this late date, Jacobs continued to use 450/17 which was marked with a fire-breathing devil's head on the sides of the fuselage. It was probably the longest-serving operational triplane, Jacobs having originally collected it as a new machine from AFP IV on 27 February.

152. Original transfer seen on many of the triplane propellers shown in the foregoing pages. The motif, coloured cream and black and measuring 11cm in diameter, is the trademark of the Axial Propellerfabrik AG of Berlin.

▲153 ▼154

153. Richthofen's red-painted 152/17 which was later exhibited in the Berlin Zeughaus Museum. The most interesting aspect of its national insignia is that it has not been changed to the improved type of Balkenkreuze of thinner proportions, introduced to Jasta 11 triplanes around mid-April 1918, but retains the original over-thick crosses. This suggests that 152/17 was no longer in first-line operational use when Richthofen was lost and would make it a ready contender for preservation. The poor adherence of the red dope on the white background of the fuselage cross has resulted in the removal of the completely enclosed white border, even revealing a part of the original 5cm-wide curved white border. It is not known when this photograph was taken, but this could have been a few months (or even longer) after the aircraft was last used, and the period and manner of its storage could explain the deterioration.

154. Press photograph showing Richthofen's 152/17 alongside Boelcke's Fokker D III 352/16 on display in the entrance hall of the Zeughaus Museum, between the wars, probably in 1938. The triplane's top wing leading-edge, right-hand aileron and rudder outline have suffered from retouching. However, other photographs of 152/17 taken at the time show that it was still in exactly the same condition as shown in the aerodrome view. It is praiseworthy that no attempt was made to renovate the aircraft or its finish, and shows the historical dedication of the Zeughaus authorities. Note the double-barrelled Gast gun with its circular magazines and telescopic sight on the pedestal on the left.

manoeuvrability has already been frequently mentioned in these pages and was described as 'fabulous' and 'colossal' by the pilots who flew it. Rudolf Stark, an experienced stationary-engined fighter pilot in Jasta 34b, had this to say about his initial triplane experience:

'Flying these new machines is at first naturally very unfamiliar. Light and sensitive, they follow the slightest movement of the controls. They climb like a lift, and in the twinkling of an eye are several hundred metres high. One can turn on a spot like a top. The operation of the rotary engine has to be learned first though, and in the beginning created some difficulties.'

Due to the Fokker Dr I's light structural weight, the gyroscopic effect of its rotary engine and the short coupled layout, as well as the short wingspan and the very effective ailerons, the triplane was extremely manoeuvrable in the rolling plane. Its right-hand turns, turning in the direction of engine rotation, due to the large amount of lift from its three wings, augmented by the lift of the aerofoil-shaped undercarriage axle fairing, were even tighter than those of the Sopwith Camel. In fact, German triplane pilots were advised if attacked by a Camel to evade it by doing right-hand turns. This manoeuvre too was the Camel's forte, but the triplane's shorter radius of turn meant that eventually the Fokker pilot would be on the tail of the Camel.

Allied pilots' statements on the Voss fight and possibly engagements with other triplanes in early 1918 had alerted the British to the triplane's power of manoeuvre, and this was apparently emphasized when reports were disseminated by RFC Intelligence. When the great British fighter pilot Edward Mannock briefed the pilots of No 74 Squadron in the spring of 1918 before they went to France, he told them: 'Don't ever attempt to dog-fight a triplane on anything like equal terms as regards height, otherwise he will get on your tail, and stay there until he shoots you down.' Mannock's advice to any such unfortunates was to stay in a vertical bank with full throttle and flick out of the turn as soon as the triplane pilot appeared to be changing his position; then 'run for home like hell, kicking your rudder hard from side to side'.

It fell to Lieutenant Ira Jones to put Mannock's advice into practice when he was caught by Leutnant Jacobs of Jasta 7 at 6,000 feet near Menin on 12 April 1918. After a circling combat of some duration, Jones did just as Mannock had preached, and due to the higher speed of his S.E.5a was able to disengage and get home. His experience is recounted in detail in *King of Air-Fighters* and in *An Air-Fighter's Scrapbook* which differ slightly in detail.* What Jones fails to mention is the direction of the defensive turn that he adopted once Jacobs' all-black triplane was on his tail. This must have been a left-hand turn in which the turning radius of the S.E.5a and Fokker Dr I was about the same. Had he gone into a right-hand turn, there is no doubt that he would have been shot down. As it was, he was lucky to get away with it, since the rotary-powered triplane, tight-turning left, could also climb when so doing – height was always the advantage sought for in such situations. This is what Jacobs wrote of the encounter in his personal diary: 'During our approach to the front we saw 7 SE which we immediately attacked. I got into a good firing position on one of them, but he didn't go down.' In fact, when Jones's aircraft was examined after the fight, it was found that it had not been hit by any of the enemy's bullets.

Pilots of No 74 Squadron had other encounters with Fokker triplanes, one of the most painful being on the morning of 8 May. This combat shows that even at this relatively late date, when the triplane was beginning to be replaced in the Jagdgeschwadern with the Fokker D VII biplane, well-handled triplanes were still a force to be reckoned with. Five S.E.5a's of 'B' Flight on an Offensive Patrol had just dropped their Cooper bombs on Menin when they were attacked out of the sun near Gheluvelt by a Kette from Jasta 26. 'Within a few seconds Stuart-Smith and Bright were going down in flames, while Piggott was going down at high speed eventually to crash in No Man's Land, uninjured, but badly shaken. Young was shot up to such an extent that he had to land at Marie Capelle aerodrome, while Kiddie's machine, which was the only one of the Flight to return to our aerodrome, was well plastered with bullet holes.' This combat started when the triplanes, flying at about 15,000 feet, dived on the British formation some 3,000 feet lower. It was short and furious, lasting only a few minutes. The Kettenfuehrer was Leutnant Fritz Loerzer, Staffelfuehrer of Jasta 26, who scored his 9th victory in the fight; other victorious pilots were Leutnant Lange, Vizefeldwebel Buder and Classen.

*In the latter account Jones confuses Jacobs with Oberleutnant Schleich, Gruja of Jagdgruppe 8 comprising Jagdstaffeln 23b, 32b, 35b and 59, equipped at the time with Albatros D Va and Pfalz D IIIa.

155. The DVL triplane 528/17 (Works No 2196) in the wooden hangar at Boeblingen during the early 1930s. It was one of the few aircraft actually assembled for display before the collection at Stuttgart was moved to Berlin in 1935. The photograph is reproduced from a postcard on sale to museum visitors at Stuttgart.

▲155

156. The DVL triplane 528/17, still fitted with its Goebel Goe II 100hp engine, was over-painted red on its return from Stuttgart and is shown here displayed at the 1936 Water and Air Sport Exhibition in Berlin, incorrectly labelled as the triplane flown by Manfred von Richthofen.

▲156　▼157

157. Following the overhaul of 528/17 by Alfred Friedrich at Straussberg, near Berlin, the lifting handles on the bottom rear longerons were refitted one bay too far aft. The Fokker loan triplane did not even have lifting handles. These anomalies help to identify the machines in photographs taken during their subsequent use.

MUSEUM PIECES

THE Berlin Zeughaus (Arsenal) was established by Prussia's first king, Friedrich I, as a depot for all kinds of weaponry, being built between the years of 1695 and 1706 by Andreas Schlueter who finished it with elaborate decoration. Later this fine building at Unter den Linden 2 became a military museum to honour German feats of arms. The first aviation exhibit was Fokker D III 352/16, the aircraft used by Hauptmann Oswald Boelcke to gain his 20th victory (the first for Jagdstaffel 2) and was made available to the museum by Kogenluft some months after Boelcke's death on 28 October 1916. Following the loss of Richthofen on 21 April 1918, it was understandable that one of his machines should also be preserved for the nation in the Zeughaus.

It is not known when this aircraft, apparently 152/17 and completely over-painted red, was given to the museum by Kogenluft, but the machine's national insignia display and manner of painting indicate that they were contemporary and not applied retrospectively. Therefore, some time after Richthofen's last victory on this machine on 18 March 1918, it was painted red and was doubtless intended for further use in its all-red scheme as Richthofen's regular aircraft. It may not have been coincidence that the last combat report referring to this aeroplane with its partial red markings was only a few days before the beginning of the March Offensive. This gives some credence to the war correspondents' statements already mentioned, and the aircraft could have been completely over-painted red by 21 March 1918. Furthermore, in the early 1930s Zeughaus officials categorically stated that the all-red aircraft in their charge was Richthofen's personal machine before it was replaced with the triplane in which he was killed.

The Zeughaus survived the Allied bombing and shelling during the Second World War but suffered considerable damage, especially during the ground fighting in 1945. Whether or not these two valuable historic aircraft were evacuated to safer surroundings earlier – as were a number of aircraft belonging to the Deutsche Luftfahrt Sammlung (German Aviation Collection – DLS), following severe bomb damage and complete loss of many of its exhibits during the night of 22/23 November 1943 – is not known. It would appear that this was not done, since frequent enquiries made by the author in the 1950s to aviation enthusiasts in Berlin and to the then Zeughaus officials indicated that the machines had been destroyed. It was said that during the occupation of Berlin, Russian troops made cooking fires from material in the Zeughaus and that this included the two aeroplanes, which by that time were already badly damaged.

Another Fokker Dr I survived the aftermath of the First World War in Germany. This was 528/17 (Works No 2196) which was apparently at Adlershof for experimental work.* There it came under the auspices of the Deutschen Versuchsanstalt fuer Luftfahrt (German Aviation Test Institute – DVL) and like some 30 other First World War aircraft, including a number of captured Allied types, escaped the destruction occasioned by the Treaty of Versailles because they were either incomplete or not airworthy; in most cases components from all these aircraft had been used for various experimental purposes. The DVL was formed in April 1912 to conduct organized research into all aspects of aviation and thus had a civil as well as a military application. During the war it came under the Idflieg department Preufanstalt und Werft and from 1 January 1917 under the more general title of Flugzeugmeisterei. Thus, when it reverted to peacetime activities, the DVL was well placed to retain the not inconsiderable Idflieg testing equipment at Adlershof and such components and engines belonging to the aircraft mentioned.

Berlin had long felt the need for an aviation museum and the main advocate for such an establishment was Hauptmann Georg Krupp. During the war he had been the Kommandeur of Riesenflugzeugabteilung 501 (Giant Aeroplane Unit – RFA) and for several years from January 1919 was the manager of the Wissenschaftliche Gesellschaft fuer Luftfahrt (Scientific Aviation Company). He also edited their official organ, *Zeitschrift fuer Flugtechnik und Motorluftschiffahrt* (Magazine for Aviation and Airship Aerial Navigation – ZFM). Contributions from the DVL appeared in this journal, and doubtless Krupp's association with the DVL paved the way for him to obtain some aviation exhibits from this source, on loan, when he organized a small aviation museum at Tempelhof aerodrome in 1925. However, space in the temporary wooden building was cramped and little expansion was possible. During the next few years, when Krupp was unemployed, he worked unceasingly to create something larger and more permanent. Then in 1929, unexpectedly, Wuerttemberg announced that it would form the Deutsche Luftfahrt Museum

---

*Acceptance-flown at Schwerin on 6 May 1918, this aircraft was in the final batch of ten triplanes, all of which were accepted that month. Eight of them were powered by the Goebel Goe II 100hp seven-cylinder engine for training duties and were presumably unarmed. 528/17 was fitted with Goe II No 18.

▲158

▲159

158. Willy Gabriel with 528/17 at Straussberg following its overhaul to airworthy condition by Alfred Friedrich for flying sequences in Karl Ritter's 1938 film 'Pour le Mérite'. The machine bears the civil registration D-EFOK at the locations on the airframe, in the proportions specified in the then current regulations, which also required that the vertical tail surface should carry the insignia of Germany's national flag (black swastika on a circular white background superimposed on a red band). In this case the rudder has been painted completely red and has the white disc/swastika marking in the centre of its area. From the appearance of the rest of the aeroplane, it has been painted in red taughtening dope and carries black registration letters; the lighter shade of the rear fuselage appears to be aluminium primer. When flown in the film mentioned, the complete aircraft was painted in different shades of green, with a degree of streaking on upper and side surfaces. Engine cowling, wheel covers and all struts were painted red, and the civil registration was carried in white in small characters on the port rear fuselage, aft of the lifting handle just above the bottom longeron. Fitted here with a 120hp Clerget engine, the massive proportions of the propeller made by Hugo Heine Propellerwerk reflect the progress made in propeller design over the previous 20 years in order correctly to match the aircraft/engine combination.

159. The two museum triplanes in the air together during the filming of 'Pour le Mérite'. The nearest machine is 528/17 (D-EFOK) and the incorrectly positioned lifting handles can be seen. This triplane's national insignia was representative, but the iron cross markings on the other aircraft were badly proportioned. The fuselage marking was obviously inspired by Ernst Udet's 'LO' motif.

160. Willy Gabriel poses with the triplane flown in the film 'D III 88', on location at Bug on the island of Ruegen in the Baltic. The Fokker inventory number for the centre wing (0303) was marked upside-down on the rear spar web and can just be seen behind the right-hand gun's rear mounting. The LMG 08/15 machine-guns are late models and the Fokker 'Durchladehebel' (loading handle) seen here was never used on production triplanes, for the simple reason that it came out too late.

▼160

(German Aviation Museum) at Stuttgart. This plan received official backing and caused the Reichsverkehrs-Ministerium (German Transport Ministry) to loan the bulk of the historical material – which was government property but until then under the administration of the DVL at Adlershof – to Stuttgart. The museum opened there on 13 July 1931, not in the hoped-for building in the city, but in a large hangar near Boeblingen aerodrome which was provided by the Deutsche Reichsbahn Direktion (German Railways Administration).

Undismayed by this turn of events, Krupp, who had long realized the limitations of the museum at Tempelhof, and sure in his conviction that Berlin should also have a representative aviation museum, obtained the use of two old hangars on the Adlershof side of Johannisthal aerodrome from the Berliner Flughafen-Gesellschaft mbH (Berlin Airport Company Ltd – BFG), the organization responsible for the management and provision of aviation facilities in the Berlin area. Although Krupp had to make do with the remnants of the DVL material, it was still possible to assemble a number of aircraft. He was also able to track down many others. Thus, when the Berliner Luftfahrt-Museum (Berlin Aviation Museum) at Johannisthal opened on 15 November 1932, some 40 aeroplanes were on show, many of them historical and including a good number of First World War aircraft. Noticeably missing was a Fokker Dr I, the DVL example having gone to Stuttgart along with 36 other machines (not all of them from the First World War period) that were in the most suitable condition to be exhibited, or at least possessing the major parts of their structures, allowing them to be assembled for display. The planned museum building in Stuttgart was still not available and the dismantled fuselages of the aircraft were arranged in two long lines, their wings propped up against the walls behind them in the Boeblingen hangar. Only the Fokker triplane was assembled and this had pride of place, raised on a small dais at the end of the building.

Krupp's energy knew no bounds when it came to finding aeroplanes suitable for his museum, and he saw the Fokker triplane as an essential display item. With this in mind he contacted Fokker in Amsterdam towards the end of 1932 and apparently asked for the loan of both a triplane and demonstration models of the Fokker machine-gun synchronization gear for his museum. The Fokker company passed the request to Anthony Fokker, then in the USA, who instructed his Amsterdam office to action the request at his (Fokker's) expense. Thus it was that two large crates containing a complete Fokker Dr I fitted with Oberursel engine No 3223 and a third crate containing the armament display models were dis-

patched from Amsterdam (insurance was the responsibility of the BFG) on 15 June 1933. The works serial number of the aircraft is not known and the machine had obviously been assembled from a variety of components that Fokker happened to have available; for example, the engine cowling was of the earlier open-fronted type common on preceding Fokker designs.

The letter of safe receipt stated that the goods had arrived in good condition and that they were already on display in the museum. The letter was dated 23 June 1933 – Krupp did not believe in wasting time! The delivery papers and accompanying letters were headed 'Berliner Flughafen-Gesellschaft mbH' and were signed by Krupp, indicating that at this time he was an employee of the BFG. The BFG became the custodian and operator of the aviation museum (it was already, by their good graces, installed in two of their hangars at Johannisthal) and their jurisdiction over aviation in Berlin thus extended not only to the aerodromes like Johannisthal, Staaken and Tempelhof, but also to aviation museums; initially that at Johannisthal, soon to be expanded and more suitably situated centrally in Berlin, instead of on the city's outskirts.

Fokker's manifest gave the value of the triplane as 7,000 guilders and the machine-gun demonstrators as 300 guilders. Several conditions were imposed during the loan: the main components of the aircraft bore Fokker's inventory identification numbers, 0301 stamped into the machine-gun mountings on the fuselage, and 0302, 0303 and 0304 painted on the top, middle and bottom wings respectively. These were not to be removed, so that Fokker would be saved customs charges on re-importing the aircraft into Holland; also, in such an eventuality, the BFG was to annotate their freight bill accordingly. In addition, one month at the latest after the receipt of instructions from Fokker, the items were to be dispatched to an address to be forwarded. It was understood that the aircraft and the gun gear demonstration models would, as arranged, be exhibited in the BFG hangars at Johannisthal and be maintained in good condition. Without Fokker's agreement in writing, they were not to be used for any other purpose and modifications to them were not to be undertaken. The BFG had already agreed to these conditions in a letter dated 3 January 1933, and the Fokker Amsterdam office had sent Fokker himself copies of these letters.

As cradle of German aviation, Johannisthal was an ideal location for an aviation museum, but it was to be too far away from the centre of population and so was poorly patronized. The situation in Stuttgart had not changed, so it was decided to create the German air

161. The Fokker Dr I triplane loaned by Anthony Fokker on display in the DLS museum in the late 1930s. It was normal practice to inscribe the aircraft exhibited in this Berlin museum as an educational aid, and that shown informs the visitor that Manfred von Richthofen was killed on 21 April 1918 in an aircraft of this type. The machine was painted all-red and was marked with the non-standard iron cross national insignia, a form of decoration inherited from the aeroplane's appearance in Herbert Maisch's 1938 film 'D III 88'. The burnished aluminium engine-turned open-fronted cowling of incorrect type for the triplane is adorned with the trademark casting of Fokker's signature.

▲161   ▼162

162. The DLS triplane was at Doeberitz on 21 April 1938 when Goering unveiled a memorial to Richthofen. Out of the picture on the right, flanking the memorial on the other side, stood a Messerschmitt Bf 109B-2, the equipment of I/JG 132 (Richthofen). Richthofen's mother and family were present and can just be seen here behind Goering.

museum in Berlin, providing easy access for airminded Berliners. The Johannisthal museum closed on 8 November 1934 and preparations were made to move to a large exhibition hall at Alt-Moabit 4–10, near the Lehrter railway station. It had fallen into disuse and had to be renovated, which took 21 months.

With Berlin now being the site of the country's national air museum, the Stuttgart aims were shelved and all the material concentrated at Boeblingen was transferred to Berlin in 1935. This encompassed the DVL aircraft, including Fokker Dr I 528/17. However, when the Deutsche Luftfahrt-Sammlung (German Aviation Collection) opened its doors on 20 June 1936, the Fokker triplane displayed was not 528/17 but the Fokker loan machine. The obvious question is why, with the return of the more authentic triplane from Stuttgart, was the Fokker loan aircraft not returned to Holland? Furthermore, for the whole period of the DLS exhibition the Fokker loan triplane was the only machine of this type to be shown. Possibly the DVL retained custody of 528/17, which was exhibited at the Wassersport und Luftsport Ausstellung (Water and Air Sport Exhibition) in 1936. The aircraft next appeared after being restored to airworthy condition by Alfred Friedrich at Straussberg and civil-registered D-EFOK when undergoing acceptance tests for flying sequences in the 1938 film 'Pour le Mérite'. The registration was particularly appropriate; it had previously been issued to a Klemm Kl 25d which was destroyed in 1936. There is no doubt that the Fokker loan triplane was also civil-registered so that it could carry out airworthy acceptance tests, and it was also flown in this film and in another 1938 release, 'D III 88'. Bearing in mind the Fokker loan conditions, was permission obtained to make this aircraft serviceable, and was clearance obtained from Fokker to fly the aircraft?

Answers to these questions are important since it is known that misuse of museum material in connection with the triplane flying for the film work resulted in Hauptmann Krupp being dismissed from his position as curator of what was then the largest, most comprehensive aviation museum in the world. It is, of course, possible that the Fokker loan triplane had in the interim become a gift to the DLS, which would negate the original loan conditions. Ex-Jagdstaffel 11 pilot Willy Gabriel, who did most of the triplane flying for these two films, maintained that this machine was a gift from Fokker and that the original intention was to borrow the museum aircraft to act as patterns so that Alfred Friedrich and his aircraft repair facility at Straussberg could construct flying copies of the triplane for film work. How it was decided to renovate and fly the original museum aircraft for this purpose is not known, but that is what happened and no copies were ever built. Since this action was known and apparently condoned by Krupp, he may have exceeded his terms of reference and permission should have been granted by some higher authority. It may have been for this reason that Krupp was relieved of his post. Engines and especially magnetos, in no small number (according to Gabriel), were used from the DLS holdings to support the triplane flying, which was punctuated by frequent engine changes when Oberursel, Gnome and Clerget rotaries were all used. This may also have jeopardized Hauptmann Krupp's position.

Even greater mystery surrounds Fokker Dr I 528/17 (D-EFOK). After the flying for 'Pour le Mérite', no further photographs or additional information have been found about this aeroplane. Gabriel stated that many pilots wanted to fly the triplanes, and a Rechlin test-pilot eventually crashed the aircraft that Gabriel had flown in the 'Pour le Mérite' flying sequences (528/17). The resulting damage may have been so severe that the aircraft was scrapped, which could explain why this machine does not appear in the later 1938 film 'D III 88', and why, when a triplane was needed for ceremonial occasions, it was the Fokker loan/gift triplane that was used – which further suggests that the more authentic 528/17 was no longer available. German accident reports for civil aircraft should clarify this point, and the Deutschen Luftfahrzeugrolle (German Civil Aircraft Register) will confirm the period of Zulassung (Certificate of Airworthiness) of this triplane and should indicate whether it was prematurely cancelled, and if so, the reason why. Furthermore, the civil registration marks allocated to the Fokker triplane from Holland (thought to have been D-EDRE) and details of its Zulassung should also be obtainable from the appropriate Luftfahrzeugrolle. Unfortunately, despite the widest search, it has not been possible to find a source for these documents. Thus, for the present at least, these questions must remain unanswered.

So the last three survivors of the legendary Fokker Dreidecker left the scene. However, components of any of them might yet re-surface; stranger things have happened in aviation history. If they do, their existence might yet help to explain the mysterious disappearance of 528/17, and/or provide proof that 152/17 was indeed salvaged despite the desperate consequences of the times, and/or expose the miracle that caused the DLS triplane to survive the destruction of its immediate surroundings by RAF Bomber Command in November 1943. Until then, it would appear that no genuine example of Fokker's V 5 triplane remains.

APPENDIXES

I. Translation of Reports Relating to Fokker Dr I Wing Failures

(1) LEUTNANT ARNTZEN 30 October 1917
Report on my observations of the crash of Leutnant Gontermann on 30 October 1917 around 4.10pm in Fokker Dr I 115/17

Leutnant Gontermann on a trial flight had reached a height of some 700 metres over the aerodrome when he performed two loops which appeared normal. Some 15 seconds after the second loop he went left into a vertical dive using left aileron and left rudder. As he did this I saw that both outer ends of the top wing were flapping. The aircraft then made an aileron turn, still going down almost vertically, during which all the ribs, fabric and, at a height of some 300 metres, the right-hand aileron flew off amid loud rattling. At a low height, Leutnant Gontermann, by using full up elevator, tried to level out without success and crashed some 60 metres from me, still nearly vertical, into the ground.

State of the Machine
Controls, except for ailerons, intact. Right aileron broken in the middle and its balance portion bent up at some 20°. Whether this bending, which is considerable, had already happened in the air or first on the ground, could not be determined. Ignition was 'on'. Top box spar remained undamaged until contact with the ground. All ribs and both wingtips had already detached in the air.

My opinion regarding the failure of the ribs is as follows: Due to the tight left turn, combined with the steep nose-down attitude of the machine, the left wingtip was subject to a force from the side. This force, which happens during every side-slip, is not allowed for in the wing construction, since there is no bracing present to counter such a side force. Apparently at the same time, the balance portion of the aileron was bent. Apart from this, since the auxiliary spar is only attached to the main box spar by seven ribs made of 1½mm plywood, failure occurred, which spread over the whole wing and resulted in the fatal crash.

Summary
The material was not faulty, there was no overstressing of the machine, rather irresponsible construction of three important parts.
Rectification must result through:
   (1) Bracing of the wingtip and ribs against side pressure.
   (2) Stronger attachment and construction of the spar to which the aileron is hinged.

(3) Strengthening of the balance portion of the ailerons.
    (signed) Arntzen
    Leutnant and Technical Officer
    Jagdstaffel 15

(2) ZAK CRASH COMMISSION
Report on the state of the crashed aircraft Dr I 115/17 of Leutnant Gontermann, Jasta 15. (+ 29 October 1917) (sic)
    La Neuville, near Marle, 2 November 1917

The eyewitness, Leutnant Arntzen, first observed the fluttering parts of the wing as the aeroplane slipped intentionally to the left. Because of this the airflow was not only from the front but on the contrary also hitting the wing from the side.

The first component to detach was the left aileron. After this the breaking away of the wing ribs was observed. Examination on site showed that the only complete part of the top wing was the wing spar. All the ribs, ailerons, wingtips and the fabric had detached in the air ('wegge-flattered' – fluttered away).

Examination of the ailerons showed that the auxiliary spar was insufficiently secured to the wingtip of the top wing. A large side pressure on the ailerons (such a pressure can exist when the aileron is deflected, as the eyewitness observed) must have caused the auxiliary spar to work loose from the wingtip, and since there is no side bracing present to cater for such an event, all the ribs broke loose in sympathy.

Quite apart from all the ribs, because the aileron-operating cables are internally situated, the breaking away of an aileron would, in general, cause the complete collapse as described above.

Necessary rectification would be to provide side bracing of the wingtip and the auxiliary spar and this would also result in strengthening the auxiliary spar itself. The individual details of the modifications will be discussed with the Company and the BA by going over the wing drawings.
(signed) Oblt d. R. Hoff   (signed) Ing Stellv Betsch
                (BA Fokker)

(3) ZAK CRASH COMMISSION
Report on the state of the Fokker Dr I aircraft in Jasta 11, Jagdgeschwader I
    Courtrai, 4 November 1917
(1) Crashed aircraft of Leutnant Pastor. Shown were: spar, left aileron. The spar no longer had any ribs; they had obviously broken away. The aileron was broken through behind the operating horn; the inner part was missing. The hinges securing the aileron to the auxiliary spar were satisfactory; a part of the auxiliary spar was still attached to a hinge. The outer end of the auxiliary spar was undamaged, but had pulled out of the wingtip. The balance portion of the aileron was bent upwards.

Cause: According to Rittmeister Freiherr von Richthofen, the aircraft was descending in a glide when it dropped its left wing and the aileron was used to correct this, whereby the aileron would be subject to a force which obviously the corner attachment between the auxiliary spar and the wingtip was not strong enough to withstand. The corner attachment became loose, then the auxiliary spar tore out and the rear ends of the ribs broke away.

(2) On an aircraft that in Freiherr von Richthofen's view had flown the most hours, the top wing was dismantled for examination and the fabric removed. It was established that the auxiliary spar was not secured sufficiently to the wingtip. The corner attachment was only lightly held by a mortise and tenon joint without a plywood gusset. The ribs were only let into the auxiliary spar by a small amount and nailed. The wing had suffered from the wet and the plywood webs had buckled. The buckling was assisted by the large round holes. It was found that the fabric was nailed on, and this nailing, bearing in mind the narrow width of the rib booms, as well as the thickness of the ribs, causes one to question the wisdom of this practice.

(3) On a further aircraft, the bottom wing was shown without fabric. The gluing of the rib webs and their booms had loosened so that the webs had come out of the booms. The triangular blocks in the corners between the rib webs and the spar were loose due to moisture. The whole wing had lost its structural integrity.

(4) On a last aircraft, the bottom wing was opened for comparison. It showed the same phenomena.

On all the wings that were opened up it was seen that the protective painting used for the spar and the ribs had not proofed these items sufficiently against the effects of moisture.

Oblt d. R. Hoff   Ing Diebel
Ing Stellv Betsch   Ing Dienst Fleckig

(4) ZAK Crash Commission

Combined report of the Crash Commission of the Fokker Dr I crashes (Ltn Gontermann, Ltn Pastor)

Courtrai, 4 November 1917

From the two attached reports and the statements of eyewitnesses, it can be seen that the reasons for the fatal crashes were as follows:

A newly recognized stress on the aileron, which can occur when the balance portion is predominantly too large, was observed during side-slipping and when gliding.

It is the opinion of the Commission that this stress can be accommodated if, during construction of the individual parts of the wing, the extreme treatment of the front (thorough soaking) is allowed for.

The Commission concludes that the Fokker Dr I is not at present usable at the front, and that the factory shall provide professional improvements without cost.

(signed) Obltn d. R. Hoff   (signed) Ing Diebel
(signed) Ing Stellv Betsch   (signed) Ing Dienst Fleckig

(5) Leutnant Arntzen's Personal Diary Entries

30 October 1917   Gontermann crashed fatally 50 metres away from me. Reason: Ribs in the top wing broke away as he descended in a vertical left-hand spiral.

2 November 1917   Today I took Fokker to see Gontermann's crash. Cause: Rib failures because of thoughtless design.

Author's Comments

Obviously Hoff and Betsch would have interrogated Arntzen to glean anything further. Comparing their report of 2 November with Arntzen's report, which was made on 30 October when the sequence of events was fresh in his mind, marked variations exist.

The only reason for confusion over which aileron detached first, is due to the fact that both ailerons came off before the aircraft actually crashed. Photographs show that the left-hand aileron was still attached to the aircraft by its operating cables, but was of course no longer capable of performing its function. From Arntzen's description, one would have expected that the first aileron to detach would have been the left-hand one, since that was the side the aircraft slipped towards, and his narrative so suggests this. Yet, twice, in his eyewitness report he identifies the detached aileron as the right-hand one. This reasoning also caused ZAK to name the left-hand aileron as the initial cause of the trouble. Its failure could be explained. The sequence of wing disintegration as described by Arntzen was now deliberately reversed by ZAK and was obviously done to reinforce their main suspicion of the attachment of the auxiliary spar to the wingtip. Considering this as the point of primary failure led ZAK to view the evidence of Pastor's wreckage in the same light, and the 'correctness' of this assumption must have been further enhanced when this structural junction in the Jasta 11 top wing, opened up for their inspection, was found to be 'not secured sufficiently'.

The complete separation of all the ribs from the spar must have been puzzling for Hoff and Betsch, and in their 2 November report they obviously felt that 'broke loose in sympathy' needed embellishment. Knowing that the aileron-operating cables were routed along the rear web of the box spar through holes in the ribs caused them to allude to the fact that when the aileron came off, the cables attached to it peeled the ribs off the spar. An essential requirement for this prognosis was the removal of the pulley bracket or its pulleys, adjacent to the aileron-operating horns. However, photographs of both the Gontermann and Pastor wreckage reveal that these outboard components of the aileron control system, where the direction of the cables change through 90° to lead aft to the operating horns on the ailerons, were still intact.

It is considered that the auxiliary spar attachment at the wingtip could not pull out as long as the rest of the wing remained intact. The reason that it had apparently 'failed' in both the Gontermann and Pastor crashes was because of the primary failures of the wing ribs, causing the disintegration of the wing structure. It was thus a secondary feature of the wing collapse, not the reason for it.

II. Original wing layout drawings of Fokker Dr I dated 18 September 1917 and strengthened wing layout drawings of Fokker Dr I dated November 1917

Note differences in the dimensions of wingspan and chord between this drawing and the previous drawing.

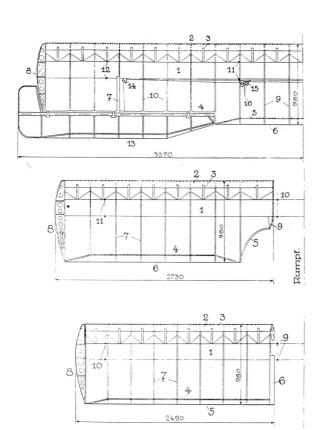

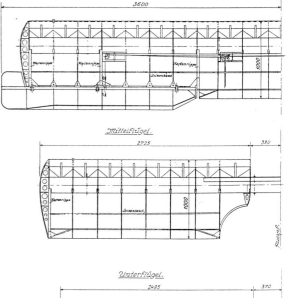

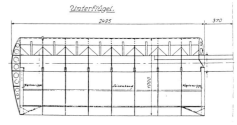

III. Technical Specification

Type: Single-seat triplane fighter
Manufacturer: Fokker Flugzeugwerke mbH, Schwerin in Mecklenburg
Manufacturer's Designation: Fokker V 5
Military Designation: Fokker Dr I

Powerplant:
Oberursel UR II 110hp 9-cylinder rotary
Oberursel UR II (Rh) 110hp 9-cylinder rotary*
(Beute-Motor) Le Rhône 110hp 9-cylinder rotary (captured engine)
Goebel Goe II 100hp 7-cylinder rotary (training aircraft only)

Dimensions
Wingspan (top), incl. aileron balances, 7.190m
Wingspan (middle) 6.225m

*Oberursel UR II built by Rhenania Motorenfabrik AG, Mannheim (Rhemag)

Wingspan (lower) 5.725m
Chord (all wings) 1.0m
Gap (middle to top) 0.875m
Gap (lower to middle) 0.855m
Aileron span 2.50m
Aileron chord (incl. balances) 0.625m*
Aileron chord (excl. balances) 0.300m
Tailplane span 2.020m
Elevator span 2.620m
Tailplane chord (max.) 1.200m
Elevator chord (incl. balances) 0.750m
Elevator chord (excl. balances) 0.424m
Fuselage, length overall 5.770m
Fuselage, length engine bulkhead to sternpost 4.490m
Height (in flying position) 2.950m
Wheel track 1.67m

*The dimensions quoted for aileron chord (incl. balances) relate to the early type aileron. Refer to wing layout drawings in this Appendix.

Areas

Top wing 7.58m^2
Middle wing 5.04m^2
Lower wing 4.86m^2
Undercarriage wing 1.18m^2
Total wing area 18.66m^2
Tailplane and elevator 2.7m^2
Rudder 0.66m^2
Ailerons (2 × 0.8m^2) 1.6m^2

Loadings

Wing loading 31.3kg/m^2
Power loading 4.5kg/hp*

*Calculated on 130bhp at 1,200rpm for Le Rhône. Oberursel UR II was less powerful: 120bhp at 1,200rpm.

Angles of Incidence

Wings (all): 2.3° positive at wing root; 2.5° positive at wingtip
Undercarriage wing axle fairing: 2° positive
Tailplane: 4.7° positive

Propeller

Two-bladed wooden construction (composition varied, usually three laminations of walnut and four laminations of birch) made by Axial Propellerwerk AG, Berlin.*

Diameter: 2.62m
Blade width: 0.23m
Pitch: 2.30m

*Propellers of similar diameter and pitch made by Hugo Heine Propellerwerk and C. Lorenzen Luftschraubenbau, both of Berlin, were also used.

Fuel and oil consumption

(Oberursel UR II at 1,200rpm)

Petrol 46 litres/hr (10.125Imp gal)
Oil 6 litres/hr (10.5Imp pints)

Magneto: Bosch ZH6

Performance

Take-off and landing runs, less than 100m
Speed in level flight at 4,000 metres altitude, 165km/hr
Ceiling, 6,000m

Climb

(Data are for Fokker Dr I 141/17 (Works No 1853) with payload of 190kg)

1,000m in approx. 2.9min
2,000m in approx. 5.5min
3,000m in approx. 9.3min
4,000m in approx. 13.9min
5,000m in approx. 21.9min

The above figures are inferior to those obtained with the modified V 4 given in the text, but it is not known what the actual weight of the modified V 4 was during the climb, although it is known that the payload was reduced to 165kg. The following data are the best recorded for the Fokker Dr I and were also achieved with a reduced payload of 165kg with 178/17 (Works No 1896):

1,000m in approx. 2.5min

2,000m in approx. 5.1min
3,000m in approx. 8.1min
4,000m in approx. 11.1min
5,000m in approx. 15.5min

Data given for 141/17 above are representative of the climbing performance of aircraft in the field, and this would doubtless worsen during service.

WEIGHT SCHEDULE

Payload (Nutzlast)	Kg
Pilot	80
2 fixed LMG 08/15 machine-guns, 11kg each	22
2 ammunition belts (500 cartridges each), 12.8kg each	25.6
Instruments and allowance for extras	11.4
Fuel and oil for 1 hour (Fuel amount reduced for acceptance flying)	41
(Full tanks 72 litres petrol and 10 litres oil = 64kg)	
Total Payload = 180kg	

Empty Weight (Powerplant)	Kg
Engine (Le Rhône 110hp)	148
Propeller and propeller hub	17
Fuel and oil tanks plus mountings (Fuel tank 72 litres capacity. Oil tank 13 litres capacity 10 litres oil and 3 litres air space)	12.9
Engine accessories (rpm indicator, fuel contents gauge, oil pulsator,* cocks, pipes, switches, etc)	16.2
Total Powerplant = 194.1kg	

*The oil pulsator was not an oil-pressure gauge but merely a sight glass connected to the delivery line from the oil pump to the engine. Each output stroke of the pump (oil pressure was only some 2psi) caused the oil level in the glass bulb to rise, falling back again on the input stroke. The rise and fall of the oil indicated the correct functioning of the oil system, and the frequency of the pulsations could be used to tell the rpm of the engine, either by entering a table or calculation; e.g., on the Oberursel UR II, 50 pulses in 30 seconds represented 1,110rpm. (The oil system was, of course, 'total loss', and the oil consumption of the engine was determined by the delivery output of the oil pump.)

Empty Weight (Airframe)	kg
Fuselage	47.3
Seat, centre-section struts, cowlings	17.5
Undercarriage, including wheels, struts, attachments and undercarriage wing	34.3
Tailskid and shock-absorber cord	1
Flying control system	3.2
Wings, complete with ailerons, hinges, interplane struts and cables, but less undercarriage wing	90
Tailplane, elevator and rudder	12.5
Fuselage fittings (e.g., machine-gun mountings)	6.1
Total Airframe = 211.9kg	
Total Empty Weight = 406.0kg	
Maximum Permissible All-Up Weight = 586.0kg	
(Empty weight for Oberursel-powered aircraft = 395.0kg)	
(Empty weight for Rhemag-powered aircraft = 386.0kg)	
(Empty weight for Goebel-powered aircraft = 392.0kg)	

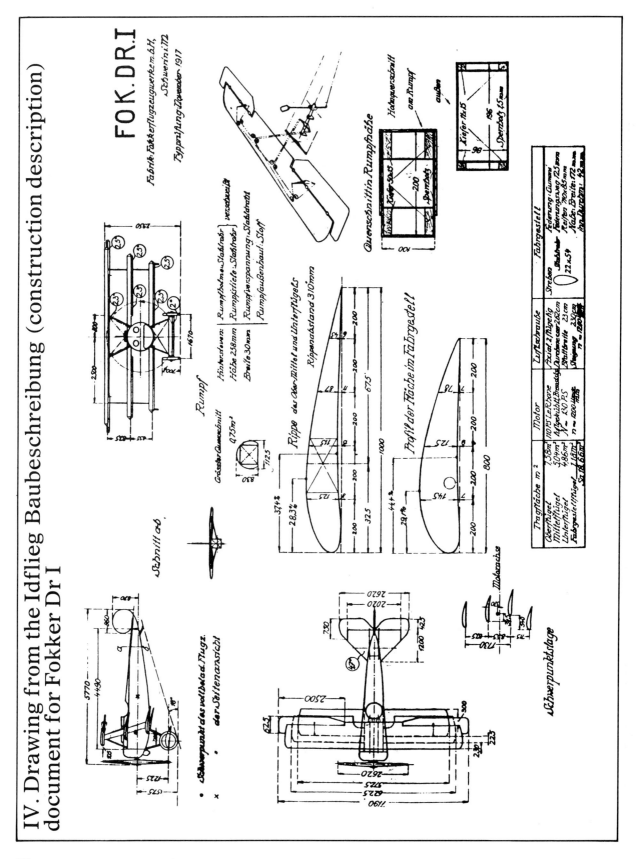

V. British contemporary general-arrangement drawing of the Fokker Dr I dated 21 May 1918.

This drawing contains some inaccuracies – e.g., the wooden interplane struts are shown here as steel struts

GENERAL ARRANGEMENT
— OF THE —
FOKKER TRIPLANE.
— SCALE ¼" = 1 FOOT —

SIDE ELEVATION.

FRONT ELEVATION.

GENERAL PLAN.

VI. Serial Numbers

German military aircraft (Fokker triplane examples are given) were required to display their military serial number painted on a vertical surface. On the triplane this was applied adjacent to the lower fuselage longerons on both sides of the fuselage between the national insignia and the cockpit. As examples in this book illustrate, serial numbers could be obliterated when pilots' identification markings were painted in this area.

The designation had to comprise the official abbreviation for the name of the manufacturer (Fok.), the official abbreviation of the aircraft class (DR I), the Bestellnummer (number of the aircraft in the order batch) and an abbreviation for the year during which the relevant order had been placed (e.g., 425/17). Since the Fokker triplanes were not all ordered at the same time, gaps in the numerical sequence of the military serial numbers of the 320 triplanes were occasioned by Idflieg reserving batches of numbers for some other manufacturers; for example, serials DR 221/17 – 399/17 were not Fokker triplanes but were numbers which were in part assigned to the Pfalz Flugzeugwerke for the intended production of their triplane.

The aircraft manufacturers had their own system of numbering aircraft during production and were required to mark this works number on all airframe components as a means of identification. Since Fokker had other aircraft types in production at the same time as the triplane, inevitably gaps were created in the sequence of works numbers assigned to the triplanes.

The following list has been compiled mainly by reference to Fokker records of aircraft accepted by Idflieg. These are unfortunately incomplete and no records are available for the months of February and March 1918. It is necessary to resort to other means in order to establish relationships between military and works numbers in the block 490/17 – 519/17 (Works No 2117–2146). The works number block quoted is based on known numbers of a ten-aircraft group in the centre of the military serial number block, which is correct for 503/17 (Works No 2130) to 512/17 (Works No 2139). This sequence has been extended outside these margins to define the limits of the relevant works numbers in this block and as a result should be used with caution. (The lower confirmed limit is 485/17 (Works No 2111), and the upper confirmed limit is 522/17 (Works No 2190), both of which are taken from Fokker records.)

Military Serial Number	Fokker Works Number
100/17	1830
101/17	1697
102/17 – 103/17	1729 – 1730
104/17 – 119/17	1772 – 1787
121/17 – 140/17	1832 – 1851
141/17 – 170/17	1853 – 1882
171/17 – 200/17	1889 – 1918
201/17 – 220/17	1920 – 1939
400/17 – 429/17	1984 – 2013
430/17 – 459/17	2055 – 2084
460/17 – 489/17	2086 – 2115
490/17 – 519/17	2117 – 2146
520/17 – 549/17	2188 – 2217
550/17 – 597/17	2220 – 2267
598/17	2269 (?)
599/17	1919

VII. Monthly Production and Front-line Strengths

The following table has been constructed from Fokker records of Idflieg Fokker triplane acceptance/dispatch data and the bi-monthly totals of the Frontbestand (front-line strengths) for the type. The incompleteness of the Fokker records is apparent. The Frontbestand figures (which are for the last day of the months given) include aircraft held at the various AFPs in readiness for distribution to units in their areas, and are thus also considered to include triplanes at Fliegerdepot Nord at Maubeuge (code-name 'Adam'). This special storage centre was established on 8 February 1918 to retain aircraft that would otherwise have been consigned to the AFP of the armies to be used in the Spring Offensive (II Armee, XVII Armee and XVIII Armee); the objective was to prevent congestion at the AFP and thus preserve their mobility so that they could be moved forward rapidly to new locations during the advance.

The Frontbestand figures do not include triplanes already accepted by Idflieg and en route to the front or those transitting Flieger Lager West at Aachen, which was the main aviation storage centre for the Western Front, and being of the 'Zwischendepot' (intermediate depot) type, its holdings were not affiliated to any particular Army.

Month	Accepted	Dispatched	Total Dispatched	Number at Front
(1917)				
Aug	2	2	2	2
Sept	12	0	2	
Oct	32	25	27	17
Nov	16	6	33	
Dec	55	49	82	35
(1918)				
Jan	54	35	117	
Feb }	125	not known	not known	143
Mar }		not known	not known	
Apr	13	not known	not known	171
May	10	not known	not known	
June				118
July				
Aug				65

VIII. Map of the Western Front showing the location of German Armies and the extent of advances made during the offensive actions of 21 March to 15 July 1918

Interpretation/Key

German front-line before 21 March 1918 ▅▅▅▅▅

German front-line achieved following various offensive actions ▅▅▅▅ ●●●●●●●

Direction of German attack thrusts ◀▅▅

Army borders ▅·▅·▅·▅

Army Group borders ▅·▅·▅·▅

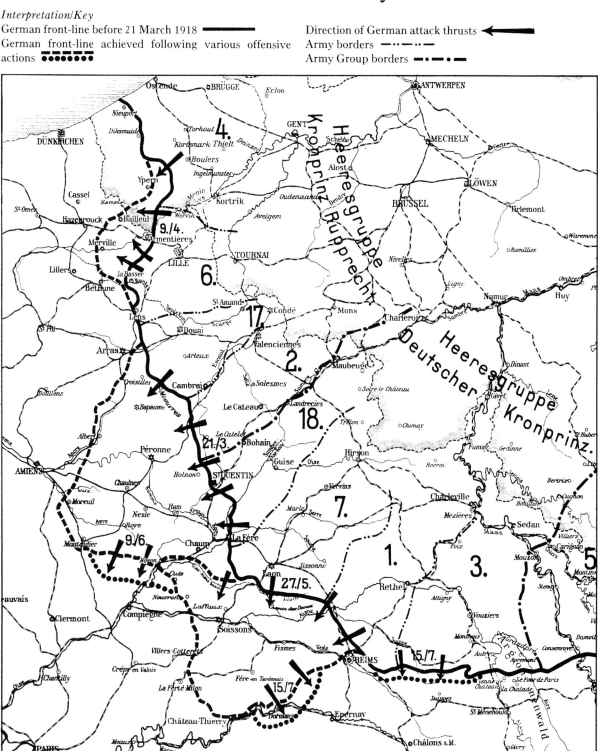

IX. Notes on Triplane Markings

1. FACTORY APPLICATION

The manner of displaying the military aircraft type designation and serial number is described in Appendix VI. The style of camouflage finish and the method of marking the national insignia are covered elsewhere and examples are shown in the photographs. The form of national insignia adhered to the instructions contained in the BLV document mentioned in the text and the method of constructing the crosses with the table of proportions provided by Idflieg is reproduced below.

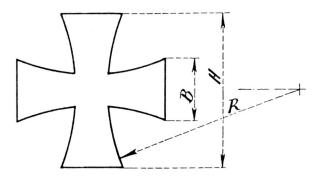

Measurements in Millimetres:

H = 1.0 H . . .	500	600	700	1,000	1,200	1,400
D = 0.4 H . . .	200	240	280	400	480	560
R = 1.3 H . . .	650	780	910	1,300	1,560	1,820

Even Idflieg instructions lacked continuity and the 'B' in the diagram, meaning Breite (width), relates to 'D' in the table meaning Durchmesser (diameter).

Works Numbers: Stencilled, usually in black on the main completed airframe components in characters 3cm high at the following locations:

Fuselage: Both sides, immediately ahead of the carburettor air intake.

Tailplane: Centre top, immediately ahead of the tailplane spar in front of the centre elevator hinge.

Elevators: Top surface, immediately aft of the operating horns.

Rudder: Both sides, at the bottom rudder bend. On late production machines, applied against a painted segment (probably dark green) at the bottom rudder outline.

Ailerons: Outboard of the centre hinge adjacent to the operating horns on the upper surfaces.

Interplane Struts: Exact location varied. Marked with abbreviations to indicate the position of the struts in the wing cellule as follows: 'U L' (Unten Links – bottom left), 'O L' (Oben Links – top left), 'U R' (Unten Rechts – bottom right) and 'O R' (Oben Rechts – top right).

Centre-section Struts: Location varied and was sometimes applied in a light colour.

Wings: All wing applications of works numbers were prefixed by the legend 'D R I' to prevent confusion with the wing number. The works number was not painted on the upper surface of the top wing, since this information already existed there (painted on the spar and visible through the celluloid window provided in the centre of the wing). However, to the immediate left of the window, the legend 'D R I' was painted on the fabric. Works numbers were applied underneath the centre-section of the top wing on the left side in line with the forward edge of the spar and at similar locations, but more outboard to clear the fuselage, on the under surfaces of the middle and lower wings.

Wing Number: The three wings were allocated their own identification number, which was the same for all the wings – i.e., the wings were a set. To prevent confusion with the works number, all references to the wing number were prefixed by an abbreviation for Flaechennummer – e.g., Fl No 1133. It was marked on the upper surface of the top wing in line with the rear edge of the spar, immediately outboard of the celluloid viewing window, and on the under surface underneath the right side of the centre-section adjacent to the forward edge of the spar. It was also marked at similar locations on the under surfaces of the middle and lower wings, but sited sufficiently outboard to clear the fuselage. (On the under wing surfaces all numbers were orientated with the leading-edges of the wings at the bottom.)

Manufacturer's Name and Aircraft Type: Motifs comprising the legend 'Fokker D R I' applied to both sides of the rudder between the two hinges adjacent to the rudder post, inside wheel covers at the tyre inflation valve apertures and at the base of all interplane strut sections.

Rigging Datum Line: A 10mm-thick black line extending aft from carburettor air intake on the thrust line for a length of 1m on each side of the fuselage.

Table of Weights: Left-hand side of the fuselage adjacent to the upper longeron and terminating in line with the centre of the cockpit. This gave weights in kilogrammes for empty weight, payload and permitted total weight and was of the following form:

Leergewicht	391kg
Nutzlast	195kg
zulässiges Gesamtgewicht	586kg

(Note: Empty weight varied depending on the type of engine fitted (see Appendix III) but was merely an average mean weight and not the true empty weight of the aircraft.)

2. UNIT MARKINGS

As examples of triplanes from each of the fourteen Jagdstaffeln considered to have operated the type as main equipment appear in the photographs in this book, the related captions contain mention of the associated unit markings. The purpose of the unit marking was to provide easy identification of the unit in the air, and to identify any aircraft as belonging to a particular unit. In large-scale formation work this allowed pilots to find their own Jagdstaffel, a function that was particularly important when re-forming after an air fight that had split up a Jagdgeschwader formation of some 50 aeroplanes.

By the time Fokker triplanes came into service, the Jagdstaffeln concerned already had a unit marking and this was, in most cases, transferred to the triplanes. A survey of a larger number of triplane photographs than could be included in this book indicates that few aircraft within a Jagdstaffel were painted in exactly the same way. The width of the stripes on tailplanes and elevators and the bands on fuselages sometimes varied quite markedly, and the amount of colour shown on the triplane noses, although generally confined to the metal engine cowling, was occasionally extended aft on the forward fuselage, sometimes as far back as the front centre-section struts. Interplane struts usually remained unpainted except in Jagdstaffeln 4, 11, 26 and 27, where it was the norm to show the unit colour on these components; but examples exist that indicate that this was not always done. It is impossible to generalize, and each triplane photograph has to be interpretated individually.

Unit Markings Summary

JG 1

Jasta 4: Engine cowling, fabric wheel covers, interplane struts in an off-white colour, exact shade not known.

Jasta 6: Engine cowling black, top and bottom surfaces of tailplane and elevators striped fore and aft in black and white.

Jasta 11: Engine cowling, interplane struts, red. (Fabric wheel covers and centre-section struts often but not invariably red.)

JG II

Jasta 12: Engine cowling white, entire rear fuselage and top and bottom surfaces of tailplane and elevators, black. (Rudder also black for a period until early April 1918.)

Jasta 13: Engine cowling white, entire rear fuselage and top and bottom surfaces of tailplane and elevators and rudder, white.

Jasta 15: Engine cowling white. Rudder only (reportedly) brown.

Jasta 19: Engine cowling white, top and bottom surfaces of tailplane and elevators (except centre of tailplane) yellow, with a broad black band on each side inclined outwards, almost parallel to the rear fuselage longerons.

JG III

Jasta Boelcke: Engine cowling black, flat front cowling face, white. Rear fuselage, top and bottom surfaces of tailplane and elevators, half black and half white, colour division on aircraft centre-line. Rudder outline sometimes with a thin black border.

Jasta 26: Engine cowling, interplane struts, black. Fuselage from cockpit aft and both surfaces of tailplane and elevators, broad black and white bands.

Jasta 27: Engine cowling, centre-section and interplane struts, rear fuselage and entire tailplane and elevators on both surfaces, yellow.

Jasta 36: Engine cowling blue. Tailplane cross (mentioned elsewhere) retained in many cases and changed to Balken-kreuz form from early April.

Non-JG Affiliated Jagdstaffeln

Jasta 14: Horizontal black and white stripe on fuselage side on thrust line from rear of engine cowling to sternpost.

Jasta 34b: Rear fuselage and complete tail unit on both top and bottom surfaces, whitish-silver. (This colour inherited from the factory finish of the unit's Pfalz D IIIa's, but reported to be with a measure of white added.)

Jasta 5: Not known with certainty that a single colour was used for unit identity. The triplanes were already decorated in either Jasta 6 or Jasta 11 markings, and these were over-painted on receipt. Whether or not an already decorated aircraft was repainted when it came on the strength of another unit was usually determined by the possible confusion that might arise if the aeroplane did not carry its own unit marking. In the case of Jasta 5 from mid-May, since it and Jasta 34b were the only triplane-operators in II Armee, there was little risk of confusion between them. Thus the possibility exists that the colours used to over-paint the Jasta 5 triplanes were varied personal colours for individual identity.

Jasta 14 was the only triplane-equipped unit in VI Armee during the summer, and there was no real need to paint a marking for unit identification on the aircraft. Indeed, a number of Jasta 14 triplanes were unmarked in this respect; by that time the unusual triplane configuration was sufficient to proclaim them as belonging to that unit. The same remarks apply to the Jasta 36 triplanes in VII Armee that lingered on until August.

3. INDIVIDUAL MARKINGS

A variety of pilots' individual markings are mentioned in the photograph captions and some explanations given concerning their origins. These markings were intended to provide immediate identification of the individual aeroplane and as such were meant to be unmistakable. The Staffelfuehrer decided whether a pilot's suggested marking was suitable for its purpose, and because of this certain trends can be identified within most units. In Jasta 11 where both surfaces of the tailplanes and elevators were used to display individual markings, the colours usually chosen were those of a pilot's previous regiment and were often also carried on the fuselage. Jasta that used tail units to show their unit marking had, perforce, to utilize the fuselage sides and decking for their individual markings, and these were often coloured bands, initial letters or other easily recognizable symbols.

Leutnant Raben caused aircraft of his command to use the symbol of a black raven, while he himself used a white raven. Although the difference in colour itself was sufficient for identification, there was another connotation in that a 'weisser Rabe' was a very rare bird indeed! (Raben's 479/17 was the only triplane in Jasta 18 and did not therefore require any special identity marking, but is mentioned here as an example only.)

Udet had carried the letters 'LO' on his aircraft since 1917, signifying the name of his fiancée (Lola), and considered this a good-luck charm, even marking it on Kirschstein's 586/17, although that aircraft's oblique black and white striping provided instant recognition and did not need any embellishment. Udet had also used a large white chevron on his aircraft after becoming the Staffelfuehrer of Jasta 37 in August 1917, and when Kirschstein's triplane was replaced by 593/17 in early June, Udet showed his chevron on the new triplane's tailplane and elevators where it would easily be seen by his pilots in the air. This was a more practical marking (commonly denoting a formation leader) than his personal 'LO', which was of course also carried. This latter marking had previously been marked as separate letters, but on 593/17 entwined letters were used in monogram form, followed by an exclamation mark, and this was the style that Udet continued to use on his later

Fokker D VII biplanes – perhaps indicating an even closer tie with Lola.

The reason why Voss displayed a decoration used on Japanese kites is thought to have been due to his contact with these because of a link, since the turn of the century, between Krefeld textile manufacturers and Japan that resulted in a number of such kites finding their way into the hands of the Krefeld businessmen's children.

So there is usually a good reason why a particular insignia was displayed by a pilot. However, many aircraft were flown already adorned with a previous pilot's marking which remained unchanged. Two examples were the Jasta 12 triplanes 217/17 (Blumenbach) and 436/17 (Hoffmann) which were still being flown by the unit in mid-June displaying the markings applied by the pilots mentioned four months earlier, both of whom were no longer in Jasta 12; Hoffmann died of wounds on 2 April and Blumenbach was posted to Jasta 31 in May.

In the Jagdstaffeln the aeroplane's individual marking belonged to the aeroplane, which could be, and frequently was, flown by a number of pilots.

INDEX

General Index

INDEX

General Index

Index of Personnel